# Contents

T0002204

# JUMBLE®
# School

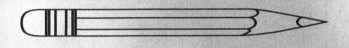

# CLASSIC
# PUZZLES

# JUMBLE.

Unscramble these four Jumbles, one letter
to each square, to form four ordinary words.

**TRUIF**

**DALLE**

**CADAFE**

**JERPUM**

SPEED
LIMIT
**50**
MPH

THE ONLY TIME
SOME DRIVERS OBEY
THE SPEED LIMIT IS
WHEN THEY'RE THIS.

Now arrange the circled letters
to form the surprise answer, as
suggested by the above cartoon.

*Print answer here*

# JUMBLE®

# School

## Puzzles for Pupils of Any Age!

**Henri Arnold,
Bob Lee,
David L. Hoyt,
and
Jeff Knurek**

TRIUMPH
B O O K S

For further information, con tact:
Triumph Books LLC
814 North Franklin Street
Chicago, Illinois 60610
Phone: (312) 337-0747
www.triumphbooks.com

Printed in U.S.A.

ISBN: 978-1-63727-328-9

Design by Sue Knopf

# JUMBLE®

Unscramble these four Jumbles, one letter to each square, to form four ordinary words.

**CELER**

**DEEXU**

**ARMKUP**

**PRAULB**

A BIRD HE SHOULD
HAVE THOUGHT
OF BEFORE HE
WAS KNOCKED OUT.

Now arrange the circled letters
to form the surprise answer, as
suggested by the above cartoon.

*Print answer here* [ ][ ][ ][ ]

# JUMBLE®

Unscramble these four Jumbles, one letter to each square, to form four ordinary words.

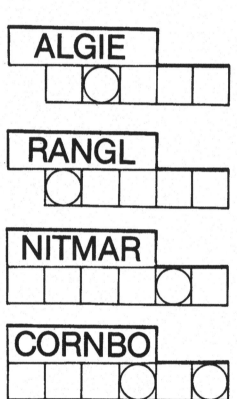

ALGIE

RANGL

NITMAR

CORNBO

HOW THE SO-CALLED "COMING" GENERATION SPENDS MUCH OF ITS TIME.

Now arrange the circled letters to form the surprise answer, as suggested by the above cartoon.

Print answer here " ☐☐☐☐☐ "

# JUMBLE®

Unscramble these four Jumbles, one letter
to each square, to form four ordinary words.

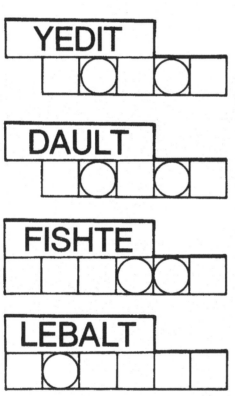

YEDIT

DAULT

FISHTE

LEBALT

And to make a
long story short. . .

Wish
he'd
come
to the
point

WHAT "TALES" TOLD BY
A LONG-WINDED BORE
USUALLY HAVE
TOO MANY OF.

Now arrange the circled letters
to form the surprise answer, as
suggested by the above cartoon.

*Print answer here* " ☐☐ – ☐☐☐☐☐ "

# JUMBLE®

Unscramble these four Jumbles, one letter
to each square, to form four ordinary words.

UMPIO

NUDAT

CAVELE

YARRIT

WHAT KIND OF
MILK DOES AN
INVISIBLE BABY
GET, NATURALLY?

Now arrange the circled letters
to form the surprise answer, as
suggested by the above cartoon.

*Print answer here*

# JUMBLE®

Unscramble these four Jumbles, one letter to each square, to form four ordinary words.

ANKEW

NEFTO

BLACOT

SLUIBY

Sign here

WHAT KIND OF INSURANCE POLICY SHOULD A SKIER TAKE OUT?

Now arrange the circled letters to form the surprise answer, as suggested by the above cartoon.

Print answer here

A " ⬡⬡⬡⬡ - ⬡⬡⬡⬡⬡ " ONE

# JUMBLE®

Unscramble these four Jumbles, one letter to each square, to form four ordinary words.

UMPEL

HOUGD

DOULCY

KABETS

WHEN HIS WIFE LOVINGLY GAVE HIM A SHIRT THAT WAS A SIZE TOO SMALL, HE GOT THIS.

Now arrange the circled letters to form the surprise answer, as suggested by the above cartoon.

**Print answer here** ALL ☐☐☐☐☐☐ ☐☐

# JUMBLE®

Unscramble these four Jumbles, one letter to each square, to form four ordinary words.

NULGE

BARIB

MOOGLY

WHAYNO

HE WAS LYING IN BED AT NIGHT THINKING OF WHAT HE HAD BEEN DOING DURING THE DAY.

Now arrange the circled letters to form the surprise answer, as suggested by the above cartoon.

*Print answer here*  ⬡⬡⬡⬡⬡

# JUMBLE®

Unscramble these four Jumbles, one letter
to each square, to form four ordinary words.

MARDA

NAKTE

TALIXY

BRUHEC

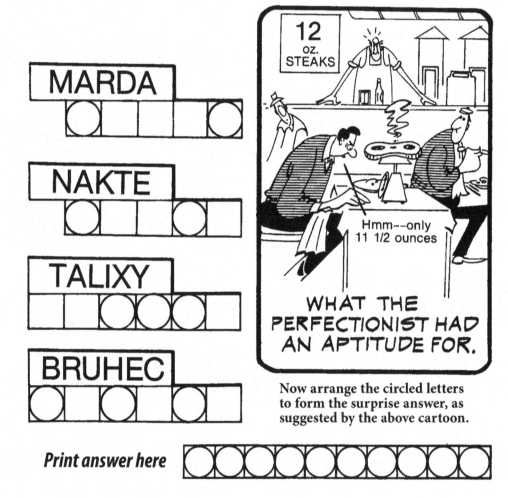

12
OZ.
STEAKS

Hmm--only
11 1/2 ounces

WHAT THE
PERFECTIONIST HAD
AN APTITUDE FOR.

Now arrange the circled letters
to form the surprise answer, as
suggested by the above cartoon.

*Print answer here*

# JUMBLE®

Unscramble these four Jumbles, one letter to each square, to form four ordinary words.

MUBAL

LULKS

NENKLE

RAUBIL

WHAT STRANGE BED-FELLOWS IN POLITICS SOON GET USED TO.

Now arrange the circled letters to form the surprise answer, as suggested by the above cartoon.

**Print answer here**  THE ⟨◯◯◯◯◯⟩ " ⟨◯◯◯◯⟩ "

# JUMBLE®

Unscramble these four Jumbles, one letter
to each square, to form four ordinary words.

SYSUF

DOGUR

JOADIN

SMARDI

You might want to
clean your room first

Are
you
kidding?!

WHAT A SPOILED
BRAT DOES.

Now arrange the circled letters
to form the surprise answer, as
suggested by the above cartoon.

**Print answer here** " ⬚⬚⬚ ' ⬚ " HIS
OWN ⬚⬚⬚

# JUMBLE®

Unscramble these four Jumbles, one letter
to each square, to form four ordinary words.

HAWTE

YUTIN

PENGOS

SMURTI

I wonder...

IT'S USUALLY
LESS THAN THE
ACTUAL COST.

Now arrange the circled letters
to form the surprise answer, as
suggested by the above cartoon.

Print
answer
here

A " ☐☐☐☐☐-☐☐☐☐☐☐ "

# JUMBLE®

Unscramble these four Jumbles, one letter
to each square, to form four ordinary words.

FLONE

SYRTT

CRADOW

BUSTIM

AT MOST BANQUETS
THIS IS THE
MAIN COURSE.

Now arrange the circled letters
to form the surprise answer, as
suggested by the above cartoon.

*Print answer here*

# JUMBLE®

Unscramble these four Jumbles, one letter to each square, to form four ordinary words.

GIMAC

BLYUL

TIBBEG

KOPHOU

I thought you knew what I wanted for breakfast

WHAT TO DO IF YOU DON'T LIKE GRANULATED SUGAR IN YOUR COFFEE.

Now arrange the circled letters to form the surprise answer, as suggested by the above cartoon.

Print answer here

# JUMBLE®

Unscramble these four Jumbles, one letter to each square, to form four ordinary words.

**MEHRY**

**NIGVY**

**SAUTLE**

**ENSTEW**

THE CONSTITUTION GUARANTEES FREE SPEECH, BUT IT DOESN'T GUARANTEE THIS.

Now arrange the circled letters to form the surprise answer, as suggested by the above cartoon.

*Print answer here*

# JUMBLE®

Unscramble these four Jumbles, one letter to each square, to form four ordinary words.

CETTO

RISUV

SUMMUE

LATBEL

They say it's a real love match

SHE MARRIED A BANKER BECAUSE HIS VIRTUES EXCEEDED THIS.

Now arrange the circled letters to form the surprise answer, as suggested by the above cartoon.

Print answer here  HIS " ○○○○○○ "

# JUMBLE®

Unscramble these four Jumbles, one letter to each square, to form four ordinary words.

LUCCK

TAPAD

DILEEY

PAMEND

SOME COMPLIMENTS ARE NOT SO MUCH CANDID AS THIS.

Now arrange the circled letters to form the surprise answer, as suggested by the above cartoon.

Print answer here "  "

# JUMBLE®

Unscramble these four Jumbles, one letter to each square, to form four ordinary words.

LYBER

YEDEK

TALKEN

DEGULC

Careful where you're driving

BANK

THE FIRST THING
A MAN OFTEN
RUNS INTO WITH
A NEW CAR.

Now arrange the circled letters to form the surprise answer, as suggested by the above cartoon.

**Print answer here** ◯◯◯◯

# JUMBLE®

Unscramble these four Jumbles, one letter to each square, to form four ordinary words.

OPUCE

PIGER

HATTOR

COIPLE

WHAT A SUCCESSFUL PICKPOCKET ALWAYS TRIES TO GET NEXT TO.

Now arrange the circled letters to form the surprise answer, as suggested by the above cartoon.

Print answer here    THE " ⬡⬡⬡⬡⬡ " ⬡⬡⬡⬡⬡⬡

# JUMBLE®

Unscramble these four Jumbles, one letter to each square, to form four ordinary words.

LEBLE

ROHTT

CAULNY

TUITOW

Closin' time

ALL-NIGHT CONVERSATIONS TEND TO BE DULLEST JUST BEFORE THIS.

Now arrange the circled letters to form the surprise answer, as suggested by the above cartoon.

*Print answer here* ⬡⬡⬡ " ⬡⬡⬡⬡ "

21

# JUMBLE®

Unscramble these four Jumbles, one letter
to each square, to form four ordinary words.

TOSOY

CLUHG

ARUSSE

LIVOAJ

Since his last birthday there's
nothing else on his mind

WHAT A BOY SCOUT
BECOMES AT A
CERTAIN AGE.

Now arrange the circled letters
to form the surprise answer, as
suggested by the above cartoon.

Print answer
here

A ◯◯◯◯ " ◯◯◯◯◯ "

# JUMBLE®

Unscramble these four Jumbles, one letter to each square, to form four ordinary words.

LAIGY

MIDIO

JELGUN

RIEVIL

HE WOULDN'T BE IN SUCH A HURRY IF HE KNEW HE WAS THIS.

Now arrange the circled letters to form the surprise answer, as suggested by the above cartoon.

Print answer here

[ ] [ ] [ ] [ ] [ ] [ ] [ ] [ ] TO [ ] [ ] [ ] [ ]

# JUMBLE®

Unscramble these four Jumbles, one letter
to each square, to form four ordinary words.

NACHT

KLAYN

CLOIPY

BELUCK

You sure charge enough!

For years I wasn't making a dime

WHAT THE
CHIROPRACTOR'S FEES
AMOUNTED TO.

Now arrange the circled letters
to form the surprise answer, as
suggested by the above cartoon.

*Print answer here* " ⃝⃝⃝⃝ " ⃝⃝⃝

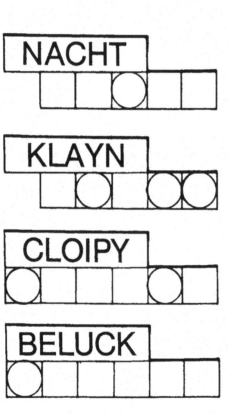

# JUMBLE®

Unscramble these four Jumbles, one letter
to each square, to form four ordinary words.

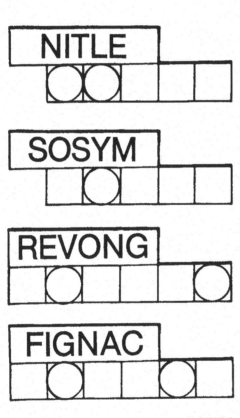

NITLE

SOSYM

REVONG

FIGNAC

...And then I went to
blah...blah...blah...

WHAT GOES ON
AND ON AND HAS
"ONESELF" IN THE
MIDDLE?

Now arrange the circled letters
to form the surprise answer, as
suggested by the above cartoon.

*Print answer here*  "  -  "

# JUMBLE®

Unscramble these four Jumbles, one letter to each square, to form four ordinary words.

COPAH

YINNF

GLAHGE

ALESEW

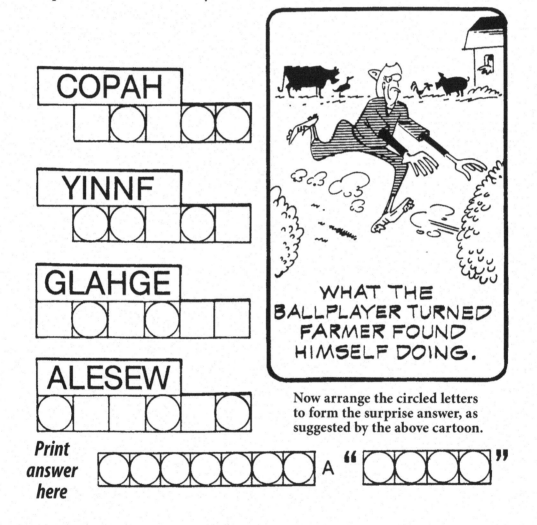

WHAT THE BALLPLAYER TURNED FARMER FOUND HIMSELF DOING.

Now arrange the circled letters to form the surprise answer, as suggested by the above cartoon.

Print answer here

A " "

# JUMBLE® School

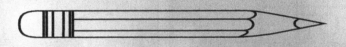

## DAILY PUZZLES

# JUMBLE®

Unscramble these four Jumbles, one letter
to each square, to form four ordinary words.

CROAH

SCOTI

THELLA

ENWAKE

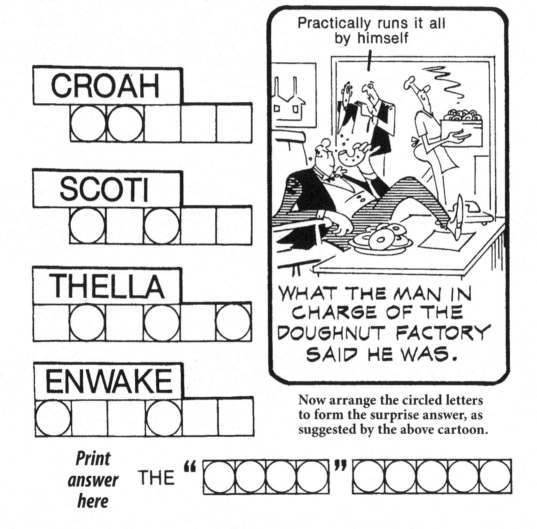

Practically runs it all
by himself

WHAT THE MAN IN
CHARGE OF THE
DOUGHNUT FACTORY
SAID HE WAS.

Now arrange the circled letters
to form the surprise answer, as
suggested by the above cartoon.

Print
answer
here

THE " ◯◯◯◯ " ◯◯◯◯◯

# JUMBLE®

Unscramble these four Jumbles, one letter
to each square, to form four ordinary words.

NUBOD

CAUDT

LYMBAC

PERREF

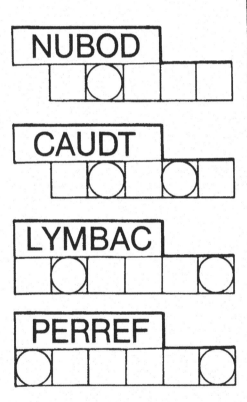

ANOTHER THING
YOU CAN'T TAKE
WITH YOU.

Now arrange the circled letters
to form the surprise answer, as
suggested by the above cartoon.

*Print answer here*

# JUMBLE®

Unscramble these four Jumbles, one letter
to each square, to form four ordinary words.

PHRAC

TELOX

HIWALE

MELING

WHAT TUNE DID
THE TEAKETTLE
WHISTLE?

Now arrange the circled letters
to form the surprise answer, as
suggested by the above cartoon.

Print
answer
here

" ⬡⬡⬡⬡ ON THE ⬡⬡⬡⬡⬡ "

# JUMBLE®

Unscramble these four Jumbles, one letter
to each square, to form four ordinary words.

ORDEN

ERECK

KLEREN

DRAFTI

THE FEAR THAT
RELATIVES ARE
COMING TO STAY.

Now arrange the circled letters
to form the surprise answer, as
suggested by the above cartoon.

**Print answer here** "◯◯◯ ◯◯◯◯◯◯"

# JUMBLE®

Unscramble these four Jumbles, one letter to each square, to form four ordinary words.

PORRI
◯◯◯◯◯

LOGAT
◯◯◯◯◯

VERYUP
◯◯◯◯◯◯

BURTAN
◯◯◯◯◯◯

HE WAS SO LAZY HE DIDN'T GIVE A RAP, EVEN WHEN THIS DID.

CHECK

Now arrange the circled letters to form the surprise answer, as suggested by the above cartoon.

**Print answer here**

◯◯◯◯◯◯◯◯◯◯◯◯◯

# JUMBLE®

Unscramble these four Jumbles, one letter to each square, to form four ordinary words.

LECCY

ADGUY

MAYLIF

EXLUDE

WHAT THAT MARRIAGE COUNSELOR WAS ALWAYS IN THE MIDDLE OF.

Now arrange the circled letters to form the surprise answer, as suggested by the above cartoon.

**Print answer here**

33

# JUMBLE®

Unscramble these four Jumbles, one letter
to each square, to form four ordinary words.

OSSUE

SYSAG

SOPHIL

INTADE

FOR THAT FANATIC
COLLECTOR, THIS
WAS AN OBSESSION.

Now arrange the circled letters
to form the surprise answer, as
suggested by the above cartoon.

**Print answer here**

# JUMBLE®

Unscramble these four Jumbles, one letter
to each square, to form four ordinary words.

NELEK

MOAXI

DAHLER

RASTIE

HIS FOOTPRINTS
ON THE SANDS OF
TIME LEFT ONLY
THIS.

Now arrange the circled letters
to form the surprise answer, as
suggested by the above cartoon.

**Print answer here**   THE ⬡⬡⬡⬡⬡ OF A ⬡⬡⬡⬡

# JUMBLE®

Unscramble these four Jumbles, one letter
to each square, to form four ordinary words.

TCHAB

PLITO

SULTYS

REHFIE

I'll never take a boat

SOME PEOPLE DON'T
TRUST THE OCEAN,
BECAUSE THEY'RE
CONVINCED THERE'S
SOMETHING ---

Now arrange the circled letters
to form the surprise answer, as
suggested by the above cartoon.

*Print
answer
here*

" ⟩⟩ IT

# JUMBLE®

Unscramble these four Jumbles, one letter
to each square, to form four ordinary words.

VARNE

CEEPI

REEVER

LIMIES

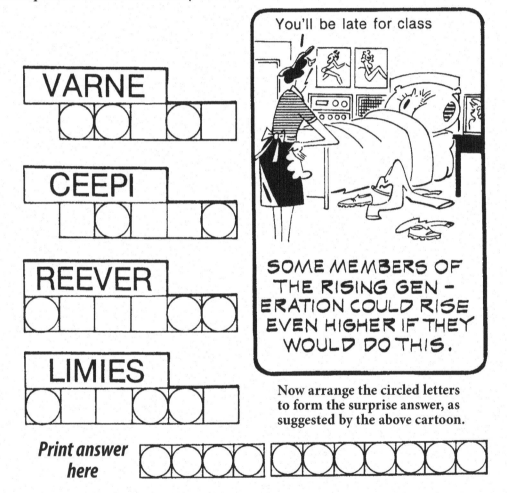

You'll be late for class

SOME MEMBERS OF
THE RISING GEN –
ERATION COULD RISE
EVEN HIGHER IF THEY
WOULD DO THIS.

Now arrange the circled letters
to form the surprise answer, as
suggested by the above cartoon.

**Print answer here**

# JUMBLE®

Unscramble these four Jumbles, one letter
to each square, to form four ordinary words.

RAYIF

VORLE

DERAAP

BIDITT

Say I'm
not in

A DEADBEAT
STICKS TO HIS
FRIENDS UNTIL THIS.

Now arrange the circled letters
to form the surprise answer, as
suggested by the above cartoon.

*Print answer
here* "⬡⬡⬡⬡" DO
THEM ⬡⬡⬡⬡

# JUMBLE®

Unscramble these four Jumbles, one letter to each square, to form four ordinary words.

TUXEL

STUMY

LYSEEP

VEEBAH

WHAT A CAR BRINGS OUT IN SOME MEN.

Now arrange the circled letters to form the surprise answer, as suggested by the above cartoon.

**Print answer here**

# JUMBLE®

Unscramble these four Jumbles, one letter to each square, to form four ordinary words.

VANIE

INFEK

COLLEA

SMUQIR

HE BELIEVED IN MARRYING A WOMAN FOR HER FIGURE, ESPECIALLY WHEN IT DID THIS.

Now arrange the circled letters to form the surprise answer, as suggested by the above cartoon.

Print answer here

INTO

# JUMBLE®

Unscramble these four Jumbles, one letter
to each square, to form four ordinary words.

INNEL

BOMUX

CRASAF

ILCAME

We're going to miss him

WHAT THEY EXPE-
RIENCED WHEN THE
LIFE OF THE PARTY
FINALLY WENT HOME.

Now arrange the circled letters
to form the surprise answer, as
suggested by the above cartoon.

Print
answer
here

" "

# JUMBLE®

Unscramble these four Jumbles, one letter
to each square, to form four ordinary words.

**TCHEF**

**EUQUE**

**NOAZAM**

**CENNAD**

FIT TO BE
EATEN EXCEPT
IN THIS.

Now arrange the circled letters
to form the surprise answer, as
suggested by the above cartoon.

*Print answer here*

# JUMBLE®

Unscramble these four Jumbles, one letter to each square, to form four ordinary words.

FORVA

VOLCE

YIFTON

TIMOON

WHAT THE BIGAMIST TOOK.

Now arrange the circled letters to form the surprise answer, as suggested by the above cartoon.

**Print answer here**

# JUMBLE®

Unscramble these four Jumbles, one letter
to each square, to form four ordinary words.

FIDUL

DEEGH

YEKTUR

TOIPLE

Boy—is he ugly!

WHAT POSITION
DOES A MONSTER
PLAY ON THE
HOCKEY TEAM?

Now arrange the circled letters
to form the surprise answer, as
suggested by the above cartoon.

**Print answer here** " ◯◯◯◯◯ – ◯◯ "

# JUMBLE®

Unscramble these four Jumbles, one letter
to each square, to form four ordinary words.

ETHAL

HALCK

RAZDAH

WUNTAL

NEEDS TO KNOW
YOUR ZODIACAL
SIGN BEFORE SHE
TELLS YOU THIS.

Now arrange the circled letters
to form the surprise answer, as
suggested by the above cartoon.

*Print answer here* WHAT YOU ☐☐☐☐ TO ☐☐☐☐

# JUMBLE®

Unscramble these four Jumbles, one letter to each square, to form four ordinary words.

**TAUCE**

**MEZIA**

**INZIAN**

**DRUTSY**

THE FAVORITE FISH AT THAT OLD RUSSIAN COURT.

Now arrange the circled letters to form the surprise answer, as suggested by the above cartoon.

*Print answer here* " ⬡⬡⬡⬡ – ⬡⬡⬡⬡⬡ "

# JUMBLE®

Unscramble these four Jumbles, one letter
to each square, to form four ordinary words.

NIMEC

LARAT

UPTYDE

ROOMAN

WHEN THE NEW
FAVORITE ARRIVED
AT THE ZOO, THERE
WAS THIS AMONG
THE KIDS.

Now arrange the circled letters
to form the surprise answer, as
suggested by the above cartoon.

*Print
answer
here*

"◯◯◯◯◯ – ◯◯◯◯◯◯"

# JUMBLE®

Unscramble these four Jumbles, one letter
to each square, to form four ordinary words.

WYLLO

HIWSS

AYGITE

TACHUG

A PIECE OF BEEF,
AND MAKE IT LEAN

Now arrange the circled letters
to form the surprise answer, as
suggested by the above cartoon.

**Print answer here** " ◯◯◯◯◯ ◯◯◯ ? "

# JUMBLE®

Unscramble these four Jumbles, one letter
to each square, to form four ordinary words.

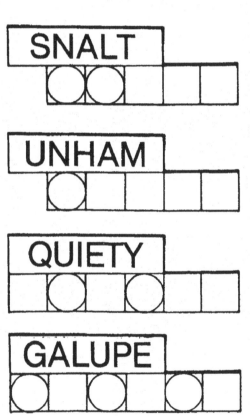

SNALT

UNHAM

QUIETY

GALUPE

Such cutting
remarks are
uncalled for

ANOTHER NAME
FOR SARCASM.

Now arrange the circled letters
to form the surprise answer, as
suggested by the above cartoon.

Print answer here  "☐☐☐☐ ☐☐☐☐"

# JUMBLE®

Unscramble these four Jumbles, one letter to each square, to form four ordinary words.

ENSOO

RIPPE

NOOMIK

THRIME

WHAT SHE THOUGHT SHE'D DO WHEN HER BOYFRIEND'S CAR NEEDED A NEW MUFFLER.

Now arrange the circled letters to form the surprise answer, as suggested by the above cartoon.

*Print answer here*

# JUMBLE®

Unscramble these four Jumbles, one letter
to each square, to form four ordinary words.

USEED

DAHYN

CAPELA

BOREEF

WHAT THE INTELLI-
GENCE AGENT HAD
WHEN HE STAYED
HOME FROM WORK.

Now arrange the circled letters
to form the surprise answer, as
suggested by the above cartoon.

Print answer
here    A " ⬡⬡⬡⬡ " IN THE ⬡⬡⬡⬡

# JUMBLE®

Unscramble these four Jumbles, one letter
to each square, to form four ordinary words.

LOBAT

TYMPE

SHAPIR

POMSIE

WHAT THE TREE
THAT EVERYONE
GATHERED UNDER
WAS CALLED.

Now arrange the circled letters
to form the surprise answer, as
suggested by the above cartoon.

*Print answer here* " ⬡⬡⬡ ' ⬡⬡⬡ "

# JUMBLE®

Unscramble these four Jumbles, one letter to each square, to form four ordinary words.

VEYHA

THOUY

SULTES

INDOWS

HIS APTITUDE FOR PLATITUDE CREATES THIS IN HIS AUDIENCE.

Now arrange the circled letters to form the surprise answer, as suggested by the above cartoon.

**Print answer here**

# JUMBLE®

Unscramble these four Jumbles, one letter
to each square, to form four ordinary words.

MORRA

CNOTH

LOWALT

DEEMLY

You're gorgeous!

Harold!

WOMEN DETEST FLAT-
TERY, ESPECIALLY
WHEN IT'S DIRECTED
TOWARDS THIS.

Now arrange the circled letters
to form the surprise answer, as
suggested by the above cartoon.

**Print answer here**

# JUMBLE®

Unscramble these four Jumbles, one letter
to each square, to form four ordinary words.

ALZEH

BOMIL

LAUTAC

NERRED

I don't see any bargains here

Looks like
a rip-off
to me

A FIRE SALE IS A
PLACE WHERE
BARGAIN HUNTERS
MIGHT GET THIS.

Now arrange the circled letters
to form the surprise answer, as
suggested by the above cartoon.

*Print answer here* "  "

# JUMBLE®

Unscramble these four Jumbles, one letter
to each square, to form four ordinary words.

BUJOM

CITOX

SHORCC

PACRIY

Tee
hee

SOMETHING OFTEN
FOUND IN NEWS-
PAPERS AND ON
BEACHES.

Now arrange the circled letters
to form the surprise answer, as
suggested by the above cartoon.

Print
answer
here

A "        "

# JUMBLE®

Unscramble these four Jumbles, one letter
to each square, to form four ordinary words.

LAFAT

YIZZD

FROMIN

TIPIDE

If you had behaved yourself, this
wouldn't have been necessary

A SURGEON MIGHT
HAVE TO CUT OUT
SOMETHING BECAUSE
THE PATIENT THIS.

Now arrange the circled letters
to form the surprise answer, as
suggested by the above cartoon.

**Print answer here**

# JUMBLE

Unscramble these four Jumbles, one letter
to each square, to form four ordinary words.

ALYMN

GLIEB

FEXNAL

TESACK

MOST PEOPLE ARE
PUT OUT WHEN
THEY'RE THIS.

Now arrange the circled letters
to form the surprise answer, as
suggested by the above cartoon.

Print answer here "  "

# JUMBLE®

Unscramble these four Jumbles, one letter to each square, to form four ordinary words.

MOVEN

SEMYS

DREHWS

LOUTTE

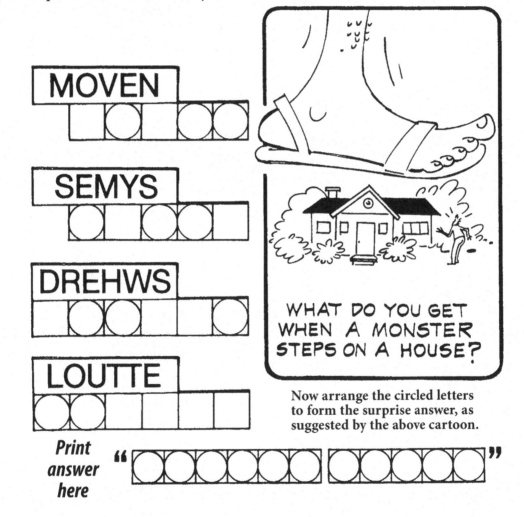

WHAT DO YOU GET WHEN A MONSTER STEPS ON A HOUSE?

Now arrange the circled letters to form the surprise answer, as suggested by the above cartoon.

Print answer here  "◯◯◯◯◯◯◯ ◯◯◯◯◯"

59

# JUMBLE®

Unscramble these four Jumbles, one letter
to each square, to form four ordinary words.

LEWJE

PLIMB

GINRAD

UNPOCE

Remember, that's supposed to be a binding agreement

JUSTICE
PEACE

WHAT A MARRIAGE
CERTIFICATE SHOULD
BE WRITTEN ON.

Now arrange the circled letters
to form the surprise answer, as
suggested by the above cartoon.

Print answer here "⬡⬡⬡⬡⬡" ⬡⬡⬡⬡⬡

# JUMBLE®

Unscramble these four Jumbles, one letter to each square, to form four ordinary words.

KAYLE

LURBY

YEUFLE

INVOIS

Freshly caught

WHAT WERE THE SHOEMAKER'S TWO FAVORITE KINDS OF FISH?

Now arrange the circled letters to form the surprise answer, as suggested by the above cartoon.

**Print answer here** ◯◯◯◯ & '◯◯◯

# JUMBLE®

Unscramble these four Jumbles, one letter
to each square, to form four ordinary words.

ZYCAR

EMARK

SETTAL

HESTOO

No ambition

And look at those shoes

WHAT LOAFERS LACK.

Now arrange the circled letters
to form the surprise answer, as
suggested by the above cartoon.

**Print answer here**

# JUMBLE®

Unscramble these four Jumbles, one letter to each square, to form four ordinary words.

KRECE

NUFNY

FIVYER

EBRTET

Let everyone know we're ready to host a housewarming party.

I'm posting it right now.

We are ready to turn your electricty on.

THEY WERE IN THE PROCESS OF TURNING ON THE HOME'S POWER, WHICH MADE IT A ---

Now arrange the circled letters to form the surprise answer, as suggested by the above cartoon.

**Print answer here**

# JUMBLE®

Unscramble these four Jumbles, one letter to each square, to form four ordinary words.

CMISU

NSALT

CUEQHN

DOWNEO

They're lucky to get all the latest fashions.

I wonder what the men's styles are going to be.

THE STORE'S WINDOW FEATURED ALL-FEMALE LIFE-SIZE FIGURES. ONE COULD CALL THEM ---

Now arrange the circled letters to form the surprise answer, as suggested by the above cartoon.

Print answer here " "

# JUMBLE®

Unscramble these four Jumbles, one letter
to each square, to form four ordinary words.

ORJEK

MICPR

PTYREO

TTTEAL

Is that my saw?

I'm going
to have
to call
you
back.

I'm glad we
finally got
our permits.

No more sharing
the bed.

THE DOGS LEARNED TO USE TOOLS
SO THEY COULD WORK ON THEIR ---

Now arrange the circled letters
to form the surprise answer, as
suggested by the above cartoon.

Print
answer
here

# JUMBLE®

Unscramble these four Jumbles, one letter to each square, to form four ordinary words.

CDNEU

CAKNK

OMUPID

CAFROT

Welcome back! You're looking good!

You look like you're back in shape.

I feel like myself again.

THE CIRCLE HAD BEEN SICK FOR A WHILE BUT WAS HAPPY TO BE ---

Now arrange the circled letters to form the surprise answer, as suggested by the above cartoon.

**Print answer here**

# JUMBLE®

Unscramble these four Jumbles, one letter to each square, to form four ordinary words.

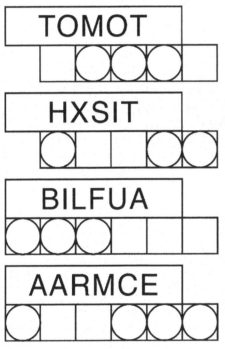

TOMOT

HXSIT

BILFUA

AARMCE

Look! My Springsteen shirt still fits!

Really, honey? It barely fit you when you bought it.

WHEN HE SAID HIS FAVORITE OLD T-SHIRT STILL FIT HIM, IT WAS A ---

Now arrange the circled letters to form the surprise answer, as suggested by the above cartoon.

**Print answer here**

# JUMBLE®

Unscramble these four Jumbles, one letter
to each square, to form four ordinary words.

DUEEL

KKONC

CPLUTS

TUEPPP

It's expensive to explore the ocean. Luckily, you have the money.

What's the use of making millions if you can't spend it?

TO BUILD A SUBMARINE
TO REACH THE OCEAN'S
LOWEST POINT, IT TOOK ---

Now arrange the circled letters
to form the surprise answer, as
suggested by the above cartoon.

**Print
answer
here**

# JUMBLE®

Unscramble these four Jumbles, one letter
to each square, to form four ordinary words.

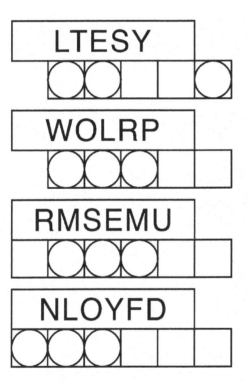

LTESY

WOLRP

RMSEMU

NLOYFD

C'mon!
Giddyup!

Hey!
Just say,
"Go faster."
No need
to poke me
without
warning.

THE HORSE DIDN'T LOVE THE
IDEA OF BEING URGED TO
SPEED UP AT THE ---

Now arrange the circled letters
to form the surprise answer, as
suggested by the above cartoon.

*Print
answer
here*

THE

# JUMBLE®

Unscramble these four Jumbles, one letter
to each square, to form four ordinary words.

HHCTU

SIHTO

LLDAYG

BRIFEB

You're welcome to take
that to a table to read it.

Thanks!
But I'm just
browsing.

SHE OPENED THE BOOK ABOUT
TREES SO SHE COULD ---

Now arrange the circled letters
to form the surprise answer, as
suggested by the above cartoon.

**Print
answer
here**

# JUMBLE®

Unscramble these four Jumbles, one letter to each square, to form four ordinary words.

PHEDT

LUCTO

GUYNHR

IERFUG

Wow! That's high-tech!

The water slices through the stone according to the computer's drawing.

THE COMPANY'S NEW FACILITY FOR PRODUCING GRANITE AND MARBLE COUNTERTOPS WAS ---

Now arrange the circled letters to form the surprise answer, as suggested by the above cartoon.

**Print answer here**

# JUMBLE®

Unscramble these four Jumbles, one letter to each square, to form four ordinary words.

RUBOR

DEUNG

OLIWLW

LGENIJ

HIS STEAK HAD BEEN COOKED THOROUGHLY, WHICH HE CONSIDERED A ---

Now arrange the circled letters to form the surprise answer, as suggested by the above cartoon.

*Print answer here*

# JUMBLE®

Unscramble these four Jumbles, one letter
to each square, to form four ordinary words.

XDEEU

KIRHE

GJEGOR

PAULRB

Another year! Bon anniversaire!

You are a super super-centenarian!

Merci, Charles.

WHEN JEANNE CALMENT TURNED
122 IN 1997, 121 WAS ---

Now arrange the circled letters
to form the surprise answer, as
suggested by the above cartoon.

**Print answer here**

73

# JUMBLE®

Unscramble these four Jumbles, one letter
to each square, to form four ordinary words.

**SEERU**

**DAAPN**

**HAWTTR**

**HOTSEO**

It's a real bargain!

Not with that noise.

Are you kidding me?

THE HOUSE WAS AVAILABLE
TO LEASE, BUT THE HIGHWAY
NEXT TO IT WAS A ---

Now arrange the circled letters
to form the surprise answer, as
suggested by the above cartoon.

Print answer here " ◯◯◯◯◯ - ◯◯◯◯ "

# JUMBLE®

Unscramble these four Jumbles, one letter
to each square, to form four ordinary words.

HMTIG

NRIYO

SALHPS

DAREDM

That's why he's
making the big bucks.

Wow! I didn't
realize how
attractive he is.

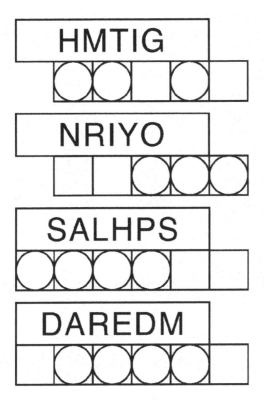

WHEN RICHARD GERE
STARRED IN THE MOVIE
"PRETTY WOMAN," HE WAS ---

Now arrange the circled letters
to form the surprise answer, as
suggested by the above cartoon.

**Print
answer
here**

# JUMBLE®

Unscramble these four Jumbles, one letter
to each square, to form four ordinary words.

SUPEA

VINGE

TANTEB

VONPER

THE MOUNTAINTOP BASKETBALL
COURT FEATURED ---

Now arrange the circled letters
to form the surprise answer, as
suggested by the above cartoon.

*Print
answer
here*

# JUMBLE®

Unscramble these four Jumbles, one letter to each square, to form four ordinary words.

NEEUV

GUHRO

GMYUSL

YAAAPP

I don't mean to talk down to you, but I'm the tallest!

I hate being in his shadow.

No one even bothers to climb me.

MOUNT EVEREST TOPS OUT AT 29,029 FEET, MAKING IT HARD FOR OTHER MOUNTAINS TO ---

Now arrange the circled letters to form the surprise answer, as suggested by the above cartoon.

*Print answer here*

# JUMBLE®

Unscramble these four Jumbles, one letter to each square, to form four ordinary words.

ARWEV

ZWTAL

HOONBB

TVANIE

It's time to hit the showers.

I'm not done! I'll change up my pitches more.

THE STARTING PITCHER ARGUED AGAINST BEING REPLACED AND DIDN'T WANT TO ---

Now arrange the circled letters to form the surprise answer, as suggested by the above cartoon.

*Print answer here*

⬡⬡⬡⬡⬡ ⬡⬡ THE ⬡⬡⬡⬡⬡

# JUMBLE®

Unscramble these four Jumbles, one letter to each square, to form four ordinary words.

MLATE

LTETI

DYOTID

SLYOSG

**Our goal is to create only the finest watches available.**

**In due course, everyone will know your name.**

ROLEX DEBUTED IN 1908 AND WOULD BECOME KNOWN FOR ITS HIGH-QUALITY WATCHES ---

Now arrange the circled letters to form the surprise answer, as suggested by the above cartoon.

*Print answer here*

◯◯◯ IN ◯◯◯◯ ◯◯◯◯

# JUMBLE®

Unscramble these four Jumbles, one letter
to each square, to form four ordinary words.

NLDEB

VHOSE

NINETV

UURXYL

Hi, I'm George Foreman, and I have a new way to cook that will knock you out.

He's the perfect spokesman.

People love him!

WHEN BOXER GEORGE FOREMAN
STARTED PROMOTING HIS
GRILL, HE BECAME A ---

Now arrange the circled letters
to form the surprise answer, as
suggested by the above cartoon.

Print
answer
here  "◯◯◯◯◯-◯◯◯◯◯◯◯"

# JUMBLE®

Unscramble these four Jumbles, one letter to each square, to form four ordinary words.

CNLIG

LNKTE

ISTAUH

CCNIES

These are all I could find to burn.

I hope we have everything. It's a long way back to the city.

CAMPERS AT THE REMOTE CAMPGROUND WERE ABLE TO BUILD A CAMPFIRE ---

Now arrange the circled letters to form the surprise answer, as suggested by the above cartoon.

Print answer here

THE

# JUMBLE®

Unscramble these four Jumbles, one letter to each square, to form four ordinary words.

PREIG

HRITS

PEPRAA

BIDYRH

The chapel of Saint Michel d'Aiguilhe is amazing! I've never seen anything like it.

It says here that, pilgrims and tourists come from all over the world to see the chapel.

WHEN THE CHURCH AT THE SUMMIT WAS VOTED "FOURTH BEST MONUMENT" IN FRANCE, IT WAS ---

Now arrange the circled letters to form the surprise answer, as suggested by the above cartoon.

*Print answer here*

 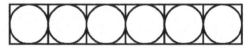

# JUMBLE®

Unscramble these four Jumbles, one letter to each square, to form four ordinary words.

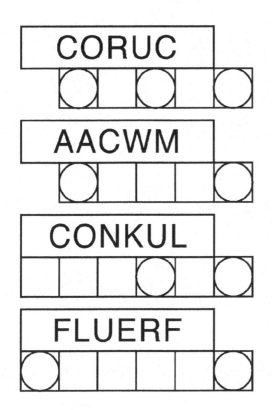

CORUC

AACWM

CONKUL

FLUERF

This is a disaster!

Clean this mess up!

Sorry. I will!

AFTER THE TEENAGER'S PARTY, HIS PARENTS WANTED HIM TO CLEAN UP THE ---

Now arrange the circled letters to form the surprise answer, as suggested by the above cartoon.

Print answer here  " ☐☐☐☐☐ "  ☐☐☐☐

# JUMBLE®

Unscramble these four Jumbles, one letter
to each square, to form four ordinary words.

ENLRI

DOYDL

MRADYE

PXOEES

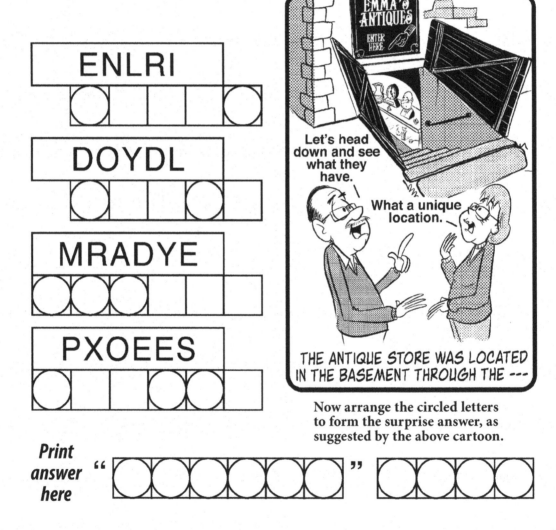

EMMA'S ANTIQUES

ENTER HERE

Let's head down and see what they have.

What a unique location.

THE ANTIQUE STORE WAS LOCATED
IN THE BASEMENT THROUGH THE ---

Now arrange the circled letters
to form the surprise answer, as
suggested by the above cartoon.

Print
answer
here "⎕⎕⎕⎕⎕⎕" ⎕⎕⎕⎕

# JUMBLE®

Unscramble these four Jumbles, one letter
to each square, to form four ordinary words.

LPXEE

TOIDT

SNYINK

LOTIVE

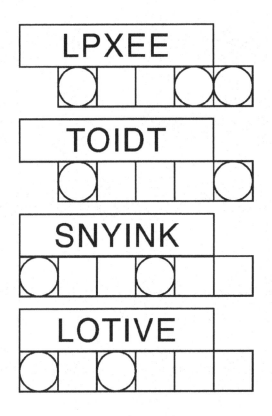

Howdy,
son!

Come give
Grammy
a hug!

Hi, Mom!

So great
to see
you!

You
haven't
changed
a bit!

THE FAMILY REUNION OF FIRST
POSITIVE NUMBERS FEATURED ---

Now arrange the circled letters
to form the surprise answer, as
suggested by the above cartoon.

*Print answer
here*

# JUMBLE®

Unscramble these four Jumbles, one letter to each square, to form four ordinary words.

**PHIOP**

**LPAYP**

**BLINEB**

**YTOPTS**

Are you okay? Do you need me to help you?

You know I haven't worked out in a while.

SHE WAS ABLE TO QUICKLY REACH THE SUMMIT BECAUSE SHE WAS ---

Now arrange the circled letters to form the surprise answer, as suggested by the above cartoon.

**Print answer here**

# JUMBLE®

Unscramble these four Jumbles, one letter to each square, to form four ordinary words.

**PDETI**

**KNAYL**

**NALSID**

**DARTIE**

We'll build right here.

You can see for miles! This is a perfect place for our new home.

WHEN THEY SETTLED WEST OF THE MISSISSIPPI, THEIR NEW HOMESTEAD WAS ---

Now arrange the circled letters to form the surprise answer, as suggested by the above cartoon.

**Print answer here**

"[ ][ ] [ ][ ][ ][ ][ ] "[ ][ ][ ][ ]""

# JUMBLE®

Unscramble these four Jumbles, one letter to each square, to form four ordinary words.

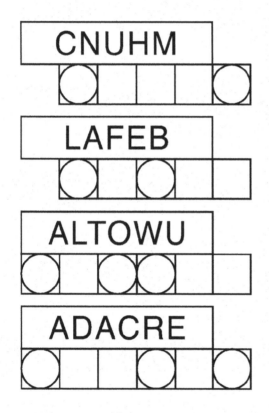

CNUHM

LAFEB

ALTOWU

ADACRE

Sonar mapping and high-tech diving vehicles have been able to measure the depths of the ocean.

Mt. Everest
4,838

6,033

I totally get it now.

USING TECHNOLOGY, DETAILS ABOUT THE DEPTH OF THE MARIANA TRENCH HAVE BECOME ---

Now arrange the circled letters to form the surprise answer, as suggested by the above cartoon.

Print answer here

# JUMBLE®

Unscramble these four Jumbles, one letter to each square, to form four ordinary words.

DFEUG

SASAL

TAGEEN

TNHISC

I'm going to get a better view!

Looks like he hasn't left the woods in months.

Will you look at that!

It's Bigfoot!

WHEN BIGFOOT WAS SPOTTED NEAR THE VILLAGE, IT ---

Now arrange the circled letters to form the surprise answer, as suggested by the above cartoon.

*Print answer here*

 “  ”

# JUMBLE®

Unscramble these four Jumbles, one letter
to each square, to form four ordinary words.

NFGLU

FIDTR

WNORAD

LODNOE

THE INITIAL INVESTORS IN
THE NEW SKYSCRAPER WERE
ABLE TO GET IN ON THE ---

Now arrange the circled letters
to form the surprise answer, as
suggested by the above cartoon.

Print
answer
here

# JUMBLE®

Unscramble these four Jumbles, one letter to each square, to form four ordinary words.

**BILAI**

**ANCET**

**TONTGE**

**PMULME**

This is the moment you've been fighting for! Are you ready?

I'm ready!

And in this corner, the challenger...

THE BOXER WAS FINALLY GIVEN A SHOT AT THE CHAMPIONSHIP, AND IT WAS ---

Now arrange the circled letters to form the surprise answer, as suggested by the above cartoon.

Print answer here " ☐-☐☐☐☐ " ☐☐☐☐

# JUMBLE®

Unscramble these four Jumbles, one letter to each square, to form four ordinary words.

**TFFHI**

**GNEBA**

**STUANN**

**GDDREE**

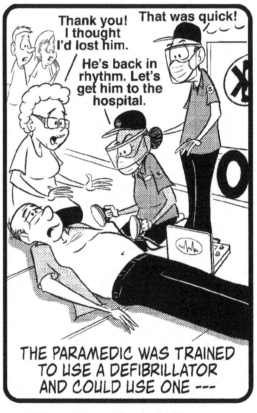

Thank you! I thought I'd lost him.

That was quick!

He's back in rhythm. Let's get him to the hospital.

THE PARAMEDIC WAS TRAINED TO USE A DEFIBRILLATOR AND COULD USE ONE ---

Now arrange the circled letters to form the surprise answer, as suggested by the above cartoon.

*Print answer here*

A

# JUMBLE®

Unscramble these four Jumbles, one letter
to each square, to form four ordinary words.

**RYOSR**

**NROTS**

**EETHLM**

**IREDIB**

See, sir? When you speak,
they immediately fall
into line.

They
better.

THE 5-FOOT-2-INCH MILITARY
LEADER GOT HIS TROOPS TO
STAND AT ATTENTION ---

Now arrange the circled letters
to form the surprise answer, as
suggested by the above cartoon.

*Print
answer
here*

# JUMBLE®

Unscramble these four Jumbles, one letter
to each square, to form four ordinary words.

HWLAS

RVEOP

TTOKYN

BEENTA

THE AUDITION WAS FOR THE LEAD
ROLE, AND THERE WERE PLENTY
OF ACTORS THERE TO ---

Now arrange the circled letters
to form the surprise answer, as
suggested by the above cartoon.

 Print answer here

# JUMBLE®

Unscramble these four Jumbles, one letter to each square, to form four ordinary words.

VASYV
◯

KANDR
◯  ◯

SUMOTC
◯  ◯

KRBEMA
◯ ◯ ◯

He has no idea about Christine's history.

This is not going to be good for him.

THE AUTOMOBILE FEATURED IN STEPHEN KING'S "CHRISTINE" HAD ---

Now arrange the circled letters to form the surprise answer, as suggested by the above cartoon.

*Print answer here* ◯◯◯ " ◯◯◯◯◯ "

# JUMBLE®

Unscramble these four Jumbles, one letter
to each square, to form four ordinary words.

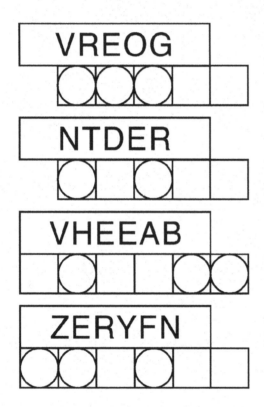

VREOG

NTDER

VHEEAB

ZERYFN

We must always
remember those who
have made the ultimate
sacrifice for our
freedoms.

Why do you
do this every
year?

REMEMBER THAT MEMORIAL
DAY IS THE LAST MONDAY IN
MAY AND YOU SHOULD ---

Now arrange the circled letters
to form the surprise answer, as
suggested by the above cartoon.

*Print
answer
here*

# JUMBLE®

Unscramble these four Jumbles, one letter to each square, to form four ordinary words.

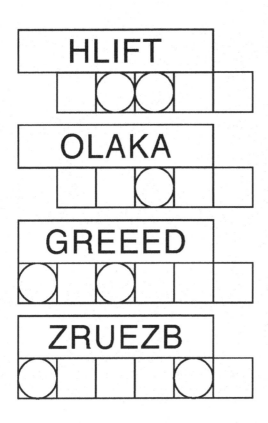

HLIFT

OLAKA

GREEED

ZRUEZB

The studio thinks this will be a huge hit.

I'm so excited about this script! I feel like a kid again.

ZOLTAR

GETTING PENNY MARSHALL TO DIRECT AND TOM HANKS TO STAR IN THE 1988 FILM WAS A ---

Now arrange the circled letters to form the surprise answer, as suggested by the above cartoon.

**Print answer here**

# JUMBLE®

Unscramble these four Jumbles, one letter
to each square, to form four ordinary words.

BEIAD

SFCOU

LEEAGB

GDEAAN

WHEN THE KIDS GOT
TOO CLOSE TO THE RIM
OF THE GRAND CANYON,
THEIR PARENTS WERE ---

Now arrange the circled letters
to form the surprise answer, as
suggested by the above cartoon.

**Print answer here**

# JUMBLE®

Unscramble these four Jumbles, one letter to each square, to form four ordinary words.

NIYCC

WYOLL

VLAREG

HELODB

This is our most-profitable drill.

The better we dig down, the higher our profits go up.

THE COMPANY SPECIALIZED IN DRILLING FOR WATER, OIL AND NATURAL GAS AND WAS ---

Now arrange the circled letters to form the surprise answer, as suggested by the above cartoon.

Print answer here

# JUMBLE®

Unscramble these four Jumbles, one letter
to each square, to form four ordinary words.

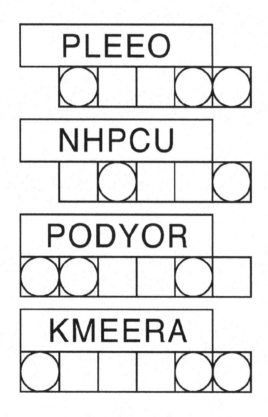

PLEEO

NHPCU

PODYOR

KMEERA

Good morning, sunshine!

There's nothing like that smell.

THE SMELL OF COFFEE
BREWING ALWAYS ---

Now arrange the circled letters
to form the surprise answer, as
suggested by the above cartoon.

Print
answer
here

# JUMBLE®

Unscramble these four Jumbles, one letter
to each square, to form four ordinary words.

**KLUSL**

**WEKAA**

**LIFTLE**

**WCRUEF**

THE DOG WAS HAVING A
PROBLEM WITH SMALL INSECTS
AND WISHED HE COULD ---

Now arrange the circled letters
to form the surprise answer, as
suggested by the above cartoon.

**Print
answer
here**

THE

# JUMBLE®

Unscramble these four Jumbles, one letter
to each square, to form four ordinary words.

INAPO

FTADR

NOOGLB

CANNEU

That homeschooling is really going well. I'm off to work.

We're moving on to the alphabet next.

1,2,3...

HE'S BEEN ABLE TO UNDERSTAND
THE MEANING OF 1, 2, 3, ETC.,
FOR A FEW MONTHS ---

Now arrange the circled letters
to form the surprise answer, as
suggested by the above cartoon.

 Print answer here

# JUMBLE

Unscramble these four Jumbles, one letter to each square, to form four ordinary words.

**TOBHO**

**ECYDA**

**SWNIEU**

**LONAGO**

I can't believe it's gone! How did this happen?

You knew this day was coming.

WHEN THE VAIN GUY LOST HIS LAST TUFT OF HAIR, ---

Now arrange the circled letters to form the surprise answer, as suggested by the above cartoon.

*Print answer here*

# JUMBLE®

Unscramble these four Jumbles, one letter to each square, to form four ordinary words.

CRATT

VAROB

ANNTTE

KOIBOE

Things are picking up.

We're starting to rake it in.

Your turn.

I'm going to double down.

BUSINESS AT THE CASINO WAS ON THE RISE AND GETTING ---

Now arrange the circled letters to form the surprise answer, as suggested by the above cartoon.

Print answer here

" ◯◯◯◯◯◯ " AND " ◯◯◯◯◯◯ "

# JUMBLE®

Unscramble these four Jumbles, one letter
to each square, to form four ordinary words.

LAMAL

DARUF

GILAOE

LANTEG

I wish this had
a heart rate
monitor on it.

They really
need to
upgrade
these. The
treads are
worn out.

THE GYM INSTALLED
SOME MEDIOCRE JOGGING
MACHINES THAT WERE ---

Now arrange the circled letters
to form the surprise answer, as
suggested by the above cartoon.

**Print
answer
here**

THE

# JUMBLE®

Unscramble these four Jumbles, one letter to each square, to form four ordinary words.

TUBAO

NAPKL

CPITKE

CAUTLA

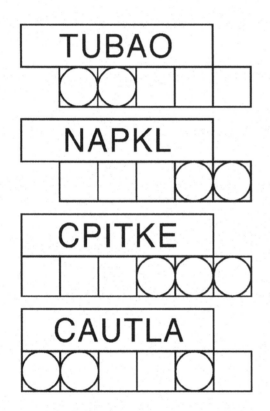

Is this a joke? Do you actually think I'm going to wear this?

Really? But it has your initial on it! I guess I'll return it.

Poi

WHEN SHE DIDN'T LIKE THE BIRTHDAY PRESENT HE GAVE HER, HE WAS ---

Now arrange the circled letters to form the surprise answer, as suggested by the above cartoon.

Print answer here

# JUMBLE®

Unscramble these four Jumbles, one letter
to each square, to form four ordinary words.

TUQSE

GILCO

GATTER

RBSBUU

When are
they going to
collect us?

We can't fit
another one
of us in
here!

FOR THE COINS IN THE
PINBALL MACHINE, IT WAS ---

Now arrange the circled letters
to form the surprise answer, as
suggested by the above cartoon.

*Print
answer
here*

# JUMBLE®

Unscramble these four Jumbles, one letter to each square, to form four ordinary words.

ORRRE

RUDGO

RWENIN

PLYOFP

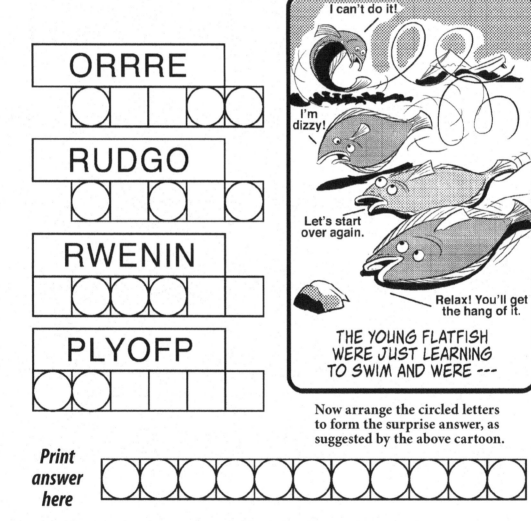

I can't do it!

I'm dizzy!

Let's start over again.

Relax! You'll get the hang of it.

THE YOUNG FLATFISH WERE JUST LEARNING TO SWIM AND WERE ---

Now arrange the circled letters to form the surprise answer, as suggested by the above cartoon.

Print answer here

# JUMBLE®

Unscramble these four Jumbles, one letter to each square, to form four ordinary words.

PGORN

PEGIR

PROEHG

ITVNEI

This is so exciting!

C'mon. Stick, you can do it!

I've never seen anything like this.

THE ARM WRESTLING MATCH HELD EVERYONE'S ATTENTION BECAUSE IT WAS ---

Now arrange the circled letters to form the surprise answer, as suggested by the above cartoon.

**Print answer here**

# JUMBLE®

Unscramble these four Jumbles, one letter
to each square, to form four ordinary words.

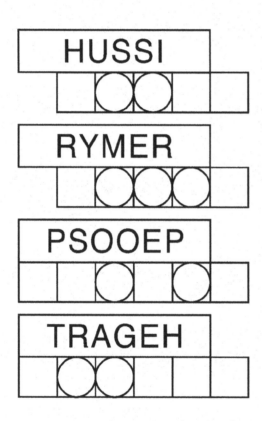

HUSSI

RYMER

PSOOEP

TRAGEH

For the Earth, the Sun is the perfect provider of heat and light.

It's amazing that if our orbit was the slightest bit off, we couldn't live here.

IT'S ONE OF BILLIONS IN THE GALAXY, BUT TO US, THE SUN IS A ---

Now arrange the circled letters
to form the surprise answer, as
suggested by the above cartoon.

**Print answer here**

# JUMBLE®

Unscramble these four Jumbles, one letter
to each square, to form four ordinary words.

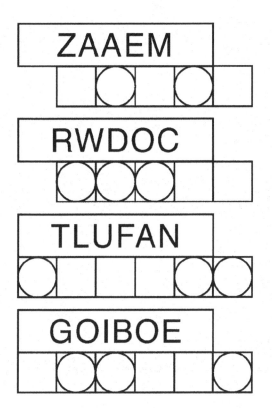

ZAEM

RWDOC

TLUFAN

GOIBOE

This new chair
is so relaxing!
I feel like I
could sit here
and talk all
day.

I want you to feel
safe and secure.
Let's get started.

THE PSYCHIATRIST'S NEW PLUSH
FURNITURE HELPED TO CREATE A ---

Now arrange the circled letters
to form the surprise answer, as
suggested by the above cartoon.

Print
answer
here

# JUMBLE®

Unscramble these four Jumbles, one letter to each square, to form four ordinary words.

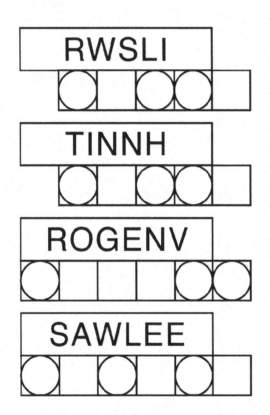

RWSLI

TINNH

ROGENV

SAWLEE

I told you two not to play back there! You'll get the rope caught in the propellor again.

Sorry. Could you help us?

THE KIDS WERE GOOFING AROUND BY THE BACK OF THE BOAT, WHICH RESULTED IN A ---

Now arrange the circled letters to form the surprise answer, as suggested by the above cartoon.

*Print answer here*

# JUMBLE®

Unscramble these four Jumbles, one letter
to each square, to form four ordinary words.

HECPE

CRSFA

LUTDON

LLRPUA

Looking good!

Thank you! My needles just fell into place tonight.

I'll take some rainwater, please.

Oh, stop it.

Aren't you looking trim tonight.

WHEN THE FOREST'S CONIFERS
HAD A PARTY, THEY GOT ---

Now arrange the circled letters
to form the surprise answer, as
suggested by the above cartoon.

*Print answer here*

# JUMBLE®

Unscramble these four Jumbles, one letter
to each square, to form four ordinary words.

MOCEA

PUSOY

RJUNIE

ZSNAAT

GOING FOR A STROLL BY
THE TOWN'S FAMOUS CLOCK
WAS A GREAT WAY TO ---

Now arrange the circled letters
to form the surprise answer, as
suggested by the above cartoon.

*Print answer here*

# JUMBLE®

Unscramble these four Jumbles, one letter
to each square, to form four ordinary words.

UDSEE

SLIBS

FLEEIN

ROHDUS

What happened to my new mirror? I can't believe this!

I'm sorry. I had trouble getting it out of the box.

WHEN SHE SAW THAT THE
BRAND-NEW MIRROR WAS
CRACKED, SHE WAS ---

Now arrange the circled letters
to form the surprise answer, as
suggested by the above cartoon.

*Print
answer
here*

# JUMBLE®

Unscramble these four Jumbles, one letter
to each square, to form four ordinary words.

BAITI

LUDWO

SOUMTT

PHREPO

What is all this? You
need to deal with this
mess right now!

Yes,
dear.

THE ATTIC WAS BECOMING
CLUTTERED, AND HIS WIFE WAS
NO LONGER GOING TO ---

Now arrange the circled letters
to form the surprise answer, as
suggested by the above cartoon.

Print
answer
here

# JUMBLE®

Unscramble these four Jumbles, one letter to each square, to form four ordinary words.

RLEDE

EEOLP

CLIEOP

LOSNDU

You'll feel the fish biting.

Then I retract the line?

Can you even eat fish?

THE ANDROID LEARNED TO FISH BY SURROUNDING HIMSELF WITH ---

Now arrange the circled letters to form the surprise answer, as suggested by the above cartoon.

**Print answer here** " ⬜⬜⬜⬜ " ⬜⬜⬜⬜⬜⬜

# JUMBLE®

Unscramble these four Jumbles, one letter
to each square, to form four ordinary words.

AQRTU

LYSET

SOCOYH

WESNRT

Sold for $1.8 million!
Wow! They were
only valued around
$9,000.

This is
incredible.

I've never
seen
anything
like this.

EINSTEIN'S HANDWRITTEN
MEMOS SOLD FOR $1.8 MILLION
BECAUSE THEY WERE ---

Now arrange the circled letters
to form the surprise answer, as
suggested by the above cartoon.

**Print
answer
here**

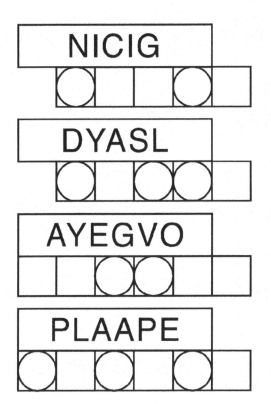

# JUMBLE®

Unscramble these four Jumbles, one letter to each square, to form four ordinary words.

NICIG

DYASL

AYEGVO

PLAAPE

Here we are, Nebraska! As far as you can see.

Welcome to NEBRASKA

It's so great to be here!

HEADING WEST FROM IOWA INTO NEBRASKA, THEY COULD SEE THE PRAIRIE ---

Now arrange the circled letters to form the surprise answer, as suggested by the above cartoon.

Print answer here

# JUMBLE®

Unscramble these four Jumbles, one letter
to each square, to form four ordinary words.

ENUQE

SAYSS

MMLUEB

LEOVRT

So, this is where it happened. The place went silent during my 10th frame.

Wow! That sounds amazing.

TO SHOW HIS GRANDSON WHERE HE BOWLED A PERFECT 300 GAME, THEY WENT TO ---

Now arrange the circled letters
to form the surprise answer, as
suggested by the above cartoon.

*Print answer here*

# JUMBLE®

Unscramble these four Jumbles, one letter to each square, to form four ordinary words.

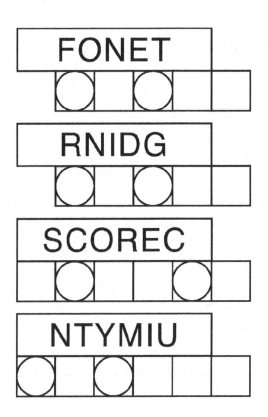

FONET

RNIDG

SCOREC

NTYMIU

You're going to love this watch.

Whoa! I'm late! Can I get the receipt?

SHE BOUGHT THE NEW WRISTWATCH, AND THEN IT WAS ---

Now arrange the circled letters to form the surprise answer, as suggested by the above cartoon.

*Print answer here*

# JUMBLE®

Unscramble these four Jumbles, one letter
to each square, to form four ordinary words.

NKLIB

TOODU

UTLNEN

ILOOER

WHEN THE STUDENT COULDN'T
GET THE MICROSCOPE TO WORK,
THE TEACHER SAID SHE'D ---

Now arrange the circled letters
to form the surprise answer, as
suggested by the above cartoon.

**Print
answer
here**

# JUMBLE®

Unscramble these four Jumbles, one letter to each square, to form four ordinary words.

CLIDH

IYDLO

TALHHE

SUEAAN

I had such a wonderful time!

Me too! We need to get back to the ship for dinner.

WHEN THEY WENT HIKING ON THE ALASKAN GLACIER, THEY ---

Now arrange the circled letters to form the surprise answer, as suggested by the above cartoon.

**Print answer here**

  "  "

# JUMBLE®

Unscramble these four Jumbles, one letter to each square, to form four ordinary words.

**PEHES**

**SRIVO**

**UUTENR**

**RMEAAC**

I can't believe we both had holes in ones!

I've never seen that happen!

They play here enough-that was bound to happen!"

TWO HOLES IN ONE IN A ROW! THE GOLFERS WERE STUNNED AT THE ---

Now arrange the circled letters to form the surprise answer, as suggested by the above cartoon.

**Print answer here**

⬡⬡⬡⬡⬡ **OF** ⬡⬡⬡⬡⬡⬡

# JUMBLE®

Unscramble these four Jumbles, one letter to each square, to form four ordinary words.

VIWEA

DLOYD

NHIYNW

GMOYSG

We brought plenty for everyone.

I'm a lefty!

Thanks for bringing all this!

Here you go!

THE KIDS WANTED TO PLAY BASEBALL. LUCKILY, THERE WERE PLENTY OF ---

Now arrange the circled letters to form the surprise answer, as suggested by the above cartoon.

Print answer here

# JUMBLE®

Unscramble these four Jumbles, one letter to each square, to form four ordinary words.

EUNOC

VGLAE

YOKEND

DLEAPD

The city is in your debt. We will name the park after you.

I just wanted to pay the city back for all the great times.

WHEN SHE SIGNED HER PROPERTY OVER TO BECOME A PARK, THEY THANKED HER FOR HER ---

Now arrange the circled letters to form the surprise answer, as suggested by the above cartoon.

**Print answer here**

# JUMBLE®

Unscramble these four Jumbles, one letter to each square, to form four ordinary words.

NTIJO

SYKAH

TBRITE

PURTAB

What did we call Magellan's route?

Pacific Ocean

Atlantic Ocean

That's what I thought.

Is it a canal or something like that?

TO NAME THE BODY OF WATER MAGELLAN TRAVELED THROUGH, SHE NEEDED TO ---

Now arrange the circled letters to form the surprise answer, as suggested by the above cartoon.

Print answer here

" "

# JUMBLE®

Unscramble these four Jumbles, one letter
to each square, to form four ordinary words.

**REUVC**

**TOHOP**

**FNELEN**

**EEESDC**

Ninety-nine more
of these and I'll
have a dollar.

x100

x4

x10

x20

I like
quarters
better.

PENNIES MAKE UP 1/100
OF A DOLLAR. THAT'S ---

Now arrange the circled letters
to form the surprise answer, as
suggested by the above cartoon.

*Print
answer
here*

# JUMBLE®

Unscramble these four Jumbles, one letter to each square, to form four ordinary words.

SEFHR

YKALE

BAREHL

ANNCNO

Are you having fun?

What a great day we're having!

This is awesome!

THEY SWAM AND BUILT A SANDCASTLE. IT WAS GOING WONDERFULLY. EVERYTHING WAS ---

Now arrange the circled letters to form the surprise answer, as suggested by the above cartoon.

Print answer here "◯◯◯◯◯◯" ◯◯◯◯

# JUMBLE®

Unscramble these four Jumbles, one letter to each square, to form four ordinary words.

RBTEE

TALGO

CYAFIP

NCRDHE

Getting all these sent out is going to be quite a feat.

With jokes like that, they should give you the boot.

Cirque Solé SHOES

THE NEW SHOE COMPANY WAS OFF TO A GREAT START AND TAKING ORDERS FOR SHOES ---

Now arrange the circled letters to form the surprise answer, as suggested by the above cartoon.

*Print answer here*

# JUMBLE®

Unscramble these four Jumbles, one letter
to each square, to form four ordinary words.

LAACN

CYTKA

BSARBO

EDMIEP

They love the
festivities.
Listen to
them go!

WHEN THE DONKEYS PARTIED LOUDLY
ON THE 4TH OF JULY, IT WAS A ---

Now arrange the circled letters
to form the surprise answer, as
suggested by the above cartoon.

Print
answer
here

" ☐☐☐☐☐ - ☐☐☐☐ - ☐☐☐☐ "

# JUMBLE®

Unscramble these four Jumbles, one letter to each square, to form four ordinary words.

GRAWE

SEHSC

TRYMOS

COYNTO

According to her grandson.

Did she really make the first flag?

Who's that?

BETSY ROSS IS CREDITED WITH MAKING THE FIRST AMERICAN FLAG, ---

Now arrange the circled letters to form the surprise answer, as suggested by the above cartoon.

Print answer here

" ☐☐☐ " THE ☐☐☐☐☐ ☐☐☐☐

# JUMBLE®

Unscramble these four Jumbles, one letter
to each square, to form four ordinary words.

RIHTD

ESBLS

KAQUWS

CRLOED

I really want
to capture
the view
from our
yard.

Our shrubs
look great.

TO COMPLETE THE PAINTING OF
THE GOLF COURSE'S THICKET,
THE ARTIST TOOK ---

Now arrange the circled letters
to form the surprise answer, as
suggested by the above cartoon.

*Print
answer
here*

# JUMBLE®

Unscramble these four Jumbles, one letter
to each square, to form four ordinary words.

PUREP

GYNTA

DIZCOA

SICAFO

Just eat
the tops as
you go.

The grass is
tickling my
tummy.

TO EAT THE SEAGRASS,
THE MANATEES ---

Now arrange the circled letters
to form the surprise answer, as
suggested by the above cartoon.

Print answer here

# JUMBLE®

Unscramble these four Jumbles, one letter to each square, to form four ordinary words.

**NIRLE**

**LAZWT**

**DMARDE**

**RNESOM**

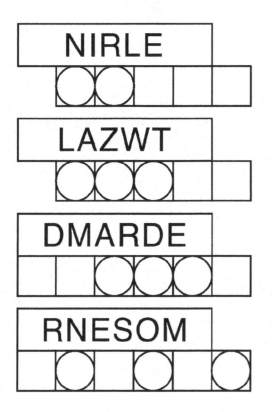

You need to follow my instructions. I don't want to see you here again.

Yes, sir.

He has no bedside manner.

Maybe. But he knows what he's doing.

THE DOCTOR HAD A ROUGH, CALLOUS BEDSIDE MANNER, BUT HE ---

Now arrange the circled letters to form the surprise answer, as suggested by the above cartoon.

**Print answer here**

# JUMBLE®

Unscramble these four Jumbles, one letter to each square, to form four ordinary words.

CTEUA

NYOEH

OEECCR

LIVJAO

As you can see, here are examples of his ability to capture historical figures, like Lincoln.

Lincoln seemed to be his specialty.

GUTZON BORGLUM'S ABILITY TO CREATE UNIQUE SCULPTURES ALLOWED HIM TO ---

Now arrange the circled letters to form the surprise answer, as suggested by the above cartoon.

**Print answer here**

# JUMBLE®

Unscramble these four Jumbles, one letter
to each square, to form four ordinary words.

ACCHO

UHESO

TNHESC

TNAFET

TOLL $3.00

Stop to pay toll ahead.

HONK!

HONK!

HONK!

It's our money! This is not funny!

This wasn't here yesterday. This is a total mess!

When did this happen?

FREE THIS BRIDGE

WHEN THEY STARTED
CHARGING A TOLL TO USE
THE BRIDGE, IT WAS A ---

Now arrange the circled letters
to form the surprise answer, as
suggested by the above cartoon.

Print answer here "◯◯◯ - ◯◯◯◯◯"

137

# JUMBLE®

Unscramble these four Jumbles, one letter
to each square, to form four ordinary words.

VIDLI

NFTOR

SOPMIE

HITIWN

I can take over from here if you'd like.

Nope! You can help me bring the table in when I'm done.

SHE HAD EVERYTHING SHE NEEDED
TO APPLY A COAT OF LACQUER
TO THE TABLE AND WOULD ---

Now arrange the circled letters
to form the surprise answer, as
suggested by the above cartoon.

Print answer here

# JUMBLE®

Unscramble these four Jumbles, one letter to each square, to form four ordinary words.

**NSYNU**

**LIOGO**

**DUEDHL**

**CNEJTI**

Can I?

First of all, it's, "May I ask a question?"

WHEN THE STUDENT SAID, "CAN I ASK A QUESTION?" THE TEACHER SAID ---

Now arrange the circled letters to form the surprise answer, as suggested by the above cartoon.

**Print answer here**

# JUMBLE®

Unscramble these four Jumbles, one letter to each square, to form four ordinary words.

IGNAA

SOGSR

NRCETH

YLASAW

Don't hurt yourself! Do you want me to get more oranges?

It's a workout! But it will all be worth it.

MAKING ALL THEIR OWN LOW-PULP ORANGE JUICE ---

Now arrange the circled letters to form the surprise answer, as suggested by the above cartoon.

Print answer here

# JUMBLE®

Unscramble these four Jumbles, one letter
to each square, to form four ordinary words.

GAEDA

RYUSL

ETAGEO

HHCATT

I think I've
cleared it
out for you.
How's that
sound?

That's
great!
Quit
talking
so
loudly.

THE PROBLEM WITH HIS
EARS WAS JUST WAX
BUILDUP, WHICH HE WAS ---

Now arrange the circled letters
to form the surprise answer, as
suggested by the above cartoon.

Print
answer
here

# JUMBLE®

Unscramble these four Jumbles, one letter
to each square, to form four ordinary words.

**SERSP**

**CRAKT**

**TOSOHM**

**VANDEI**

How have you been? I haven't seen you on the trails for a while.

I guess we just keep missing each other.

THE HIKERS HADN'T SEEN EACH OTHER IN YEARS UNTIL THEY ---

Now arrange the circled letters
to form the surprise answer, as
suggested by the above cartoon.

*Print
answer
here*

# JUMBLE®

Unscramble these four Jumbles, one letter to each square, to form four ordinary words.

DICEH

SHURC

STARHH

EEGGAN

How could you have gotten poison ivy there? You haven't been out.

I have no idea!

I'm heading to the woods! Who's been wearing my hat?

HOW HE ENDED UP WITH POISON IVY ON HIS SCALP WAS A ---

Now arrange the circled letters to form the surprise answer, as suggested by the above cartoon.

Print answer here

◯◯◯◯ - ◯◯◯◯◯◯◯◯◯◯

# JUMBLE®

Unscramble these four Jumbles, one letter to each square, to form four ordinary words.

PLAAH

PIYML

LONREL

TRABET

Zero seconds plus zero seconds equals what?

So, let's say the clocks both start at zero.

That's nothing!

HE WAS ABLE TO UNDERSTAND THE CONCEPT OF ZERO SECONDS IN ---

Now arrange the circled letters to form the surprise answer, as suggested by the above cartoon.

Print answer here

# JUMBLE ®

Unscramble these four Jumbles, one letter to each square, to form four ordinary words.

**SUYFS**

**KVOEE**

**LUTEML**

**THROTE**

What's for dessert?

I'd say we got our money's worth.

I'm stuffed!

THE RESTAURANT'S
ALL-YOU-CAN-EAT BUFFET
WAS BEING ENJOYED---

Now arrange the circled letters to form the surprise answer, as suggested by the above cartoon.

*Print answer here*

# JUMBLE®

Unscramble these four Jumbles, one letter
to each square, to form four ordinary words.

UNEEV

FEYBE

INCIOC

SNIVHA

SHE DIDN'T PLAN ON PURCHASING
A LOTTERY TICKET, BUT DID IT ---

Now arrange the circled letters
to form the surprise answer, as
suggested by the above cartoon.

**Print answer here** " ◯◯◯ " ◯◯◯◯◯◯◯

146

# JUMBLE

Unscramble these four Jumbles, one letter
to each square, to form four ordinary words.

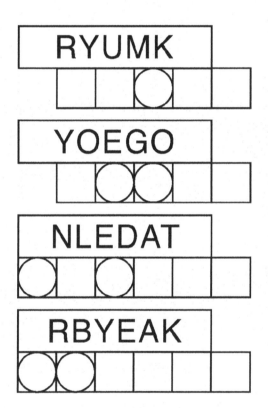

RYUMK

YOEGO

NLEDAT

RBYEAK

Can I interest either of you in a game?

Sorry, I'm headed to the pool.

Maybe after I tour the bridge.

HE WANTED TO PLAY CHESS BUT
NEEDED TO GET AN OPPONENT ---

Now arrange the circled letters
to form the surprise answer, as
suggested by the above cartoon.

**Print answer here**

147

# JUMBLE®

Unscramble these four Jumbles, one letter
to each square, to form four ordinary words.

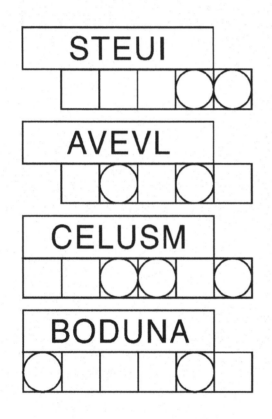

**STEUI**

**AVEVL**

**CELUSM**

**BODUNA**

It's certainly move-in ready.

When can we move in?

It's available now!

THEY WENT TO VIEW THE
EMPTY APARTMENT AND
WERE HAPPY WITH THE ---

Now arrange the circled letters
to form the surprise answer, as
suggested by the above cartoon.

**Print
answer
here**

# JUMBLE®

Unscramble these four Jumbles, one letter to each square, to form four ordinary words.

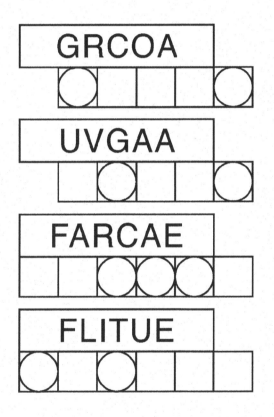

GRCOA

UVGAA

FARCAE

FLITUE

Do you know what two plus two is?

She knows her addition.

I know that! Here, see?

WHEN ASKED IF SHE KNEW WHAT TWO PLUS TWO EQUALED, SHE SAID SHE KNEW ---

Now arrange the circled letters to form the surprise answer, as suggested by the above cartoon.

Print answer here

" ⬡⬡⬡⬡ " ⬡ ⬡⬡⬡⬡

# JUMBLE®

Unscramble these four Jumbles, one letter to each square, to form four ordinary words.

IGSEN

OSUDE

MLINEB

KTHSEC

This will be perfect for your awards show.

I'll be a sharp dressed man!

THE TUXEDO LOOKED GREAT ON HIM AND WOULD PERFECTLY ---

Now arrange the circled letters to form the surprise answer, as suggested by the above cartoon.

**Print answer here**

# JUMBLE®

Unscramble these four Jumbles, one letter to each square, to form four ordinary words.

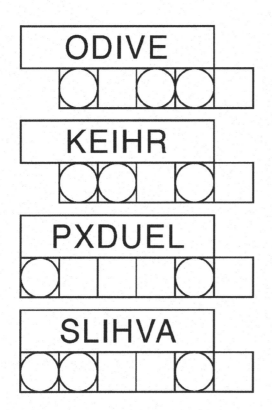

ODIVE

KEIHR

PXDUEL

SLIHVA

This will be perfect for my comic book collection!

Let's hold off and shop around.

30% OFF!

HE WANTED TO BUY THE BOOKCASE, BUT HIS WIFE ---

Now arrange the circled letters to form the surprise answer, as suggested by the above cartoon.

Print answer here

◯◯◯◯◯◯◯ THE ◯◯◯◯

# JUMBLE®

Unscramble these four Jumbles, one letter to each square, to form four ordinary words.

**EIGMA**

**PMYET**

**AANOST**

**MOOABB**

I got you!

Alright, alright! You all better run!

IF YOU GET TAGGED WHILE PLAYING TAG, JUST ACCEPT THE FACT AND THINK ---

Now arrange the circled letters to form the surprise answer, as suggested by the above cartoon.

*Print answer here*

# JUMBLE®

Unscramble these four Jumbles, one letter
to each square, to form four ordinary words.

**SPEIO**

**VLEBE**

**DYOLEM**

**ALIPSR**

I can cut your
taxes and
reduce the debt
with ease!

That's not
going to fix
anything.

Why should
we believe
him this
time?

THE POLITICIAN'S WORDS COULDN'T
BE TRUSTED, AND THEREIN ---

Now arrange the circled letters
to form the surprise answer, as
suggested by the above cartoon.

*Print
answer
here*

**THE**

# JUMBLE®

Unscramble these four Jumbles, one letter to each square, to form four ordinary words.

ALGEI

BROTI

XTCEEI

FONETS

IN ORDER TO PINPOINT THE PROBLEM, THE AUTO MECHANIC NEEDED TO ---

Now arrange the circled letters to form the surprise answer, as suggested by the above cartoon.

Print answer here

# JUMBLE®

Unscramble these four Jumbles, one letter
to each square, to form four ordinary words.

UMYGM

PMILE

HNIKRS

LRYASA

Whoa!

Oops!

Uh oh!

THE SOLDIERS BUILDING
THE NEW ARMY EATING
FACILITY WERE ---

Now arrange the circled letters
to form the surprise answer, as
suggested by the above cartoon.

*Print
answer
here*

# JUMBLE®

Unscramble these four Jumbles, one letter to each square, to form four ordinary words.

RYOEF

VOLNE

DLOYEM

RIPITS

I've got another one!

I need to upgrade my equipment.

You got your money's worth.

THE FISHING ROD AND REEL PERFORMED SO WELL BECAUSE THEY WERE ---

Now arrange the circled letters to form the surprise answer, as suggested by the above cartoon.

*Print answer here*

THE

# JUMBLE®

Unscramble these four Jumbles, one letter to each square, to form four ordinary words.

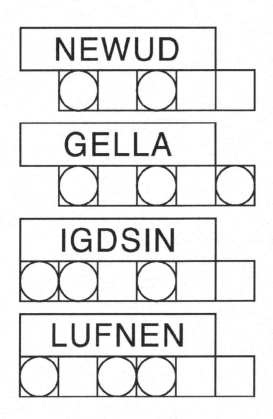

NEWUD

GELLA

IGDSIN

LUFNEN

He's going to have to catch up to the leaders.

He crushed it!

Get in the hole!

THE GOLF TOURNAMENT BEGAN ON TIME AND WAS NOW ---

Now arrange the circled letters to form the surprise answer, as suggested by the above cartoon.

*Print answer here*

# JUMBLE®

Unscramble these four Jumbles, one letter
to each square, to form four ordinary words.

NWTIE

HNISY

YARNCO

DEMLDI

Can I get some that are
holding on to each other?

SALE!

How
old are
these?
I think
these
are for
hitch-
hiking?

SOME OF THE MANNEQUIN PARTS HAD
BEEN USED FOR YEARS AND WERE ---

Now arrange the circled letters
to form the surprise answer, as
suggested by the above cartoon.

*Print
answer
here*

# JUMBLE®

Unscramble these four Jumbles, one letter
to each square, to form four ordinary words.

**XITSY**

**LNSTA**

**TEIPCO**

**LLBOGA**

IF YOU WANT TO KNOW IF DOGS
ARE HAPPY, LOOK FOR ---

Now arrange the circled letters
to form the surprise answer, as
suggested by the above cartoon.

*Print
answer
here*

⬜⬜⬜⬜ - " ⬜⬜⬜⬜ " ⬜⬜⬜⬜⬜

# JUMBLE®

Unscramble these four Jumbles, one letter
to each square, to form four ordinary words.

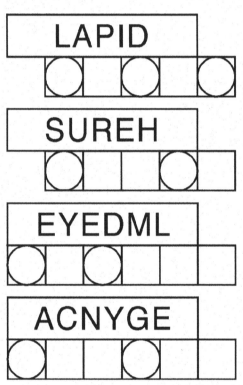

LAPID

SUREH

EYEDML

ACNYGE

Why are you awake so early?

I have a big presentation this morning.

THE ADVERTISING EXECUTIVE
WAS ANXIOUS TO GET OUT OF
BED SO SHE COULD GET ---

Now arrange the circled letters
to form the surprise answer, as
suggested by the above cartoon.

**Print
answer
here**

  "  " '

# JUMBLE®

Unscramble these four Jumbles, one letter to each square, to form four ordinary words.

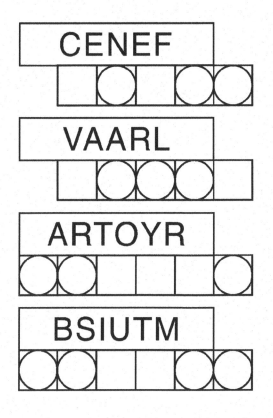

CENEF

VAARL

ARTOYR

BSIUTM

I am ready to go. I hope the congregation is ready for me.

Thank you! You've got a great crowd this morning.

THE DEACON INTRODUCED HERSELF TO THE CHURCH'S MINISTER BY SAYING ---

Now arrange the circled letters to form the surprise answer, as suggested by the above cartoon.

*Print answer here*

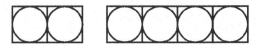

# JUMBLE®

Unscramble these four Jumbles, one letter to each square, to form four ordinary words.

**MIRGE**

**THHUC**

**SWRULA**

**TOSEOH**

They're making progress.

We should be on the other side today.

THEY STARTED WORK ON THE MOUNTAIN TUNNEL AND WOULD WORK UNTIL THEY ---

Now arrange the circled letters to form the surprise answer, as suggested by the above cartoon.

**Print answer here**

# JUMBLE® School

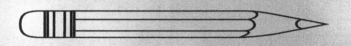

# CHALLENGER
# PUZZLES

# JUMBLE®

Unscramble these six Jumbles, one letter to each square, to form six ordinary words.

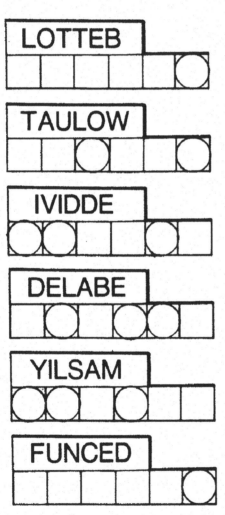

LOTTEB

TAULOW

IVIDDE

DELABE

YILSAM

FUNCED

WHAT A BELLY DANCER CAN BE EXPECTED TO DO.

Now arrange the circled letters to form the surprise answer, as suggested by the above cartoon.

**Print answer here**

⭘⭘⭘⭘⭘⭘⭘ HER ⭘⭘⭘⭘⭘⭘⭘

# JUMBLE®

Unscramble these six Jumbles, one letter to each square, to form six ordinary words.

UNBOYT

MIULEH

BABRYC

SOLANG

REKALT

TAPHAY

MAY I INTRODUCE YOU TO MY HUSBAND?

Now arrange the circled letters to form the surprise answer, as suggested by the above cartoon.

**Print answer here**

" ⬡⬡⬡⬡ " ⬡ A ⬡⬡⬡ OF ⬡⬡⬡⬡ "

# JUMBLE®

Unscramble these six Jumbles, one letter
to each square, to form six ordinary words.

BOLGEN

NUCHAH

YONNAC

FEWLOU

DOONBY

GRAFOE

WHY YOU SHOULD
GET UP BEFORE
DAYLIGHT WHEN YOU'RE
TRYING TO FIND THE
ANSWER TO A
TOUGH PROBLEM.

Now arrange the circled letters
to form the surprise answer, as
suggested by the above cartoon.

**Print answer here**

IT'LL
SOON

# JUMBLE®

Unscramble these six Jumbles, one letter
to each square, to form six ordinary words.

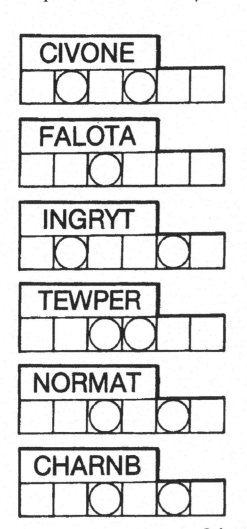

CIVONE

FALOTA

INGRYT

TEWPER

NORMAT

CHARNB

YOU SHOULD TAKE
A NUMBER AT THAT
POPULAR PASTRY
SHOP IN ORDER TO
KEEP THIS.

Now arrange the circled letters
to form the surprise answer, as
suggested by the above cartoon.

*Print answer here*

YOUR "◯◯◯◯◯" UNDER ◯◯◯◯◯◯◯◯

# JUMBLE®

Unscramble these six Jumbles, one letter to each square, to form six ordinary words.

STELEN

LAYGEL

HUTORF

MICOPY

REBLUT

THECCI

COULD THIS BE ANOTHER NAME FOR ALL THE MAIL THAT'S ON ITS WAY TO THOSE CONGRESSMEN?

Now arrange the circled letters to form the surprise answer, as suggested by the above cartoon.

**Print answer here**

" ☐☐☐☐☐☐☐ " ☐☐☐☐☐☐☐☐

# JUMBLE®

Unscramble these six Jumbles, one letter to each square, to form six ordinary words.

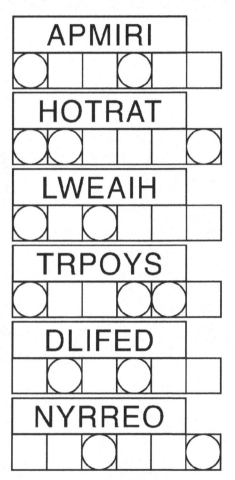

APMIRI

HOTRAT

LWEAIH

TRPOYS

DLIFED

NYRREO

I'm pretty sure I have the winner. I'm all in.

Mike, you never go all in! There's no way you're bluffing! I fold.

He usually folds.

THE POKER PLAYER HAD NEVER GONE "ALL IN" BEFORE BUT WAS NOW READY TO ---

Now arrange the circled letters to form the surprise answer, as suggested by the above cartoon.

*Print answer here*

# JUMBLE®

Unscramble these six Jumbles, one letter to each square, to form six ordinary words.

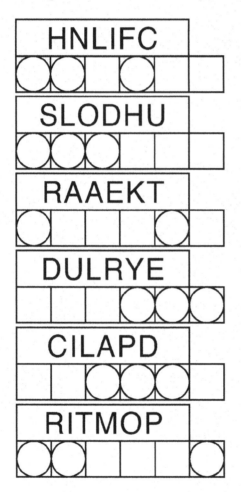

HNLIFC

SLODHU

RAAEKT

DULRYE

CILAPD

RITMOP

I love that we spend so much time together.

My mother taught me how to make these sweaters, and now I've taught the both of you.

I love it too.

THREE GENERATIONS KNEW HOW TO MAKE SWEATERS BY HAND IN THIS ---

Now arrange the circled letters to form the surprise answer, as suggested by the above cartoon.

**Print answer here**

" ⬡⬡⬡⬡⬡⬡⬡ - ⬡⬡⬡⬡⬡ " ⬡⬡⬡⬡⬡⬡

# JUMBLE®

Unscramble these six Jumbles, one letter to each square, to form six ordinary words.

SNSAOE

CRAIGL

SSEVUR

LONELP

NLAHED

CEITKL

I've got some more for you. How's it going?

Great! I'm just making sure the stems are all tied together.

THEY JUST RECEIVED MORE CELERY AND ASPARAGUS, SO THE STORE EMPLOYEE ---

Now arrange the circled letters to form the surprise answer, as suggested by the above cartoon.

**Print answer here**

" ☐☐ - ☐☐☐☐☐☐☐ " THE ☐☐☐☐☐☐☐

# JUMBLE®

Unscramble these six Jumbles, one letter to each square, to form six ordinary words.

CLUEKB

SCTTHI

EEEDCX

TINKET

SLFEUU

RZHADA

I'm so glad we were able to get outside today and enjoy the weather.

Me too, Dad! I want to be the same as you when I can ride a bike!

THE BOY AND HIS DAD BOTH ENJOYED BRIGHT, CLEAR DAYS. IT WAS ---

Now arrange the circled letters to form the surprise answer, as suggested by the above cartoon.

**Print answer here**

# JUMBLE®

Unscramble these six Jumbles, one letter to each square, to form six ordinary words.

ANGUAI

LITUAR

SYFOLT

YATARS

SLIVHA

STIFYE

You gold medals are the stars of my new display. Enjoy your new home.

SHE HUNG UP HER GOLD MEDALS BEFORE THE OTHERS BECAUSE SHE WANTED TO PUT ---

Now arrange the circled letters to form the surprise answer, as suggested by the above cartoon.

*Print answer here*

# JUMBLE®

Unscramble these six Jumbles, one letter
to each square, to form six ordinary words.

VIEIDD

SMTUPE

IMRFNO

INTTAA

NNCAYO

GLHEGA

ELIZABETH II HAS BEEN
QUEEN FOR 68 YEARS,
WHICH MAKES HER THE ---

Now arrange the circled letters
to form the surprise answer, as
suggested by the above cartoon.

*Print answer here*

# JUMBLE®

Unscramble these six Jumbles, one letter to each square, to form six ordinary words.

SANGSI

DIALSN

SMEEAS

TDOSED

RRUUMM

SAYILE

USING DRONES TO DELIVER THE MAGAZINES ---

Now arrange the circled letters to form the surprise answer, as suggested by the above cartoon.

*Print answer here*

# JUMBLE®

Unscramble these six Jumbles, one letter to each square, to form six ordinary words.

NTOHYR

BNTETI

TAHHER

MMEAYH

UQLESE

FATALO

EVEN WITHOUT A PERSONALITY, SODIUM CHLORIDE IS ---

Now arrange the circled letters to form the surprise answer, as suggested by the above cartoon.

*Print answer here*

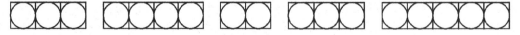

# JUMBLE®

Unscramble these six Jumbles, one letter to each square, to form six ordinary words.

UUTOGD

HALWET

DIBSEE

SFINOU

TNDOEE

GLUEED

This has cost way more than I thought it would. I really need you to win.

I'll ride as best I can to help.

AFTER BUYING SO MANY HORSES, THE OWNER OF THE HORSE FARM WAS ---

Now arrange the circled letters to form the surprise answer, as suggested by the above cartoon.

*Print answer here*

# JUMBLE®

Unscramble these six Jumbles, one letter to each square, to form six ordinary words.

SREYDS

TARIPE

TLEAYL

GRANDO

WDHAOS

ISHMYW

AFTER THE REIGNING HOT DOG-EATING CHAMPION LOST, HE ---

Now arrange the circled letters to form the surprise answer, as suggested by the above cartoon.

## Print answer here

# JUMBLE®

Unscramble these six Jumbles, one letter to each square, to form six ordinary words.

DNEATV

LMGEBA

WDEPOR

SREYDS

NYLUUR

DLNNAI

Sorry for being late.

That's OK! I haven't started yet. Let's catch some fish!

HE WAS VERY ANXIOUS FOR HIS FISHING BUDDY TO ARRIVE. HE WAS --

Now arrange the circled letters to form the surprise answer, as suggested by the above cartoon.

*Print answer here*

# JUMBLE®

Unscramble these six Jumbles, one letter to each square, to form six ordinary words.

CROADC

PITAUO

OHARTT

GNSUUF

GOILBE

AGSINS

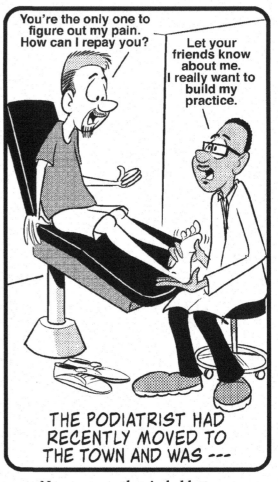

You're the only one to figure out my pain. How can I repay you?

Let your friends know about me. I really want to build my practice.

THE PODIATRIST HAD RECENTLY MOVED TO THE TOWN AND WAS ---

Now arrange the circled letters to form the surprise answer, as suggested by the above cartoon.

**Print answer here**

# JUMBLE®

Unscramble these six Jumbles, one letter
to each square, to form six ordinary words.

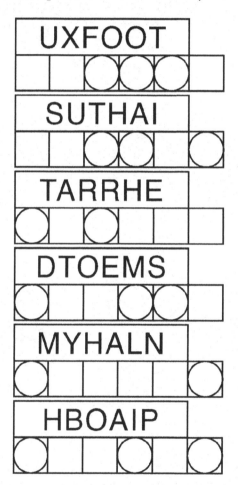

UXFOOT

SUTHAI

TARRHE

DTOEMS

MYHALN

HBOAIP

Nobel had over 350
patents. The most
famous is for dynamite,
which hasn't changed
since 1867.

Whoa! You
just blew my
mind.

He invented
dynamite that
long ago?

WHEN THEY LEARNED THAT
ALFRED NOBEL INVENTED
DYNAMITE, IT WAS A ---

Now arrange the circled letters
to form the surprise answer, as
suggested by the above cartoon.

*Print answer here*

# JUMBLE®

Unscramble these six Jumbles, one letter to each square, to form six ordinary words.

DOINGI

RSYEEG

SWYLLO

SACOIN

NEUVEA

TOHBCL

As you can see, I've gone through this again and again to reach my theory.

It looks thoroughly thought-out to me.

EINSTEIN'S THEORIES WERE PRESENTED IN SUCH DETAIL BECAUSE HE WANTED TO ---

Now arrange the circled letters to form the surprise answer, as suggested by the above cartoon.

**Print answer here**

# JUMBLE®

Unscramble these six Jumbles, one letter to each square, to form six ordinary words.

BRIELG

VIRRED

ISGTED

OLATFA

NGUYRH

LUDNAO

We're sorry we can't have a proper party for you right now. Better safe than sorry.

Such a modern celebration!

Hi, Mom! Hi, Dad! You figured it out! Good to see you.

Thanks for being here!

ON SEPTEMBER 6, 2020, SHE TURNED 18, ---

Now arrange the circled letters to form the surprise answer, as suggested by the above cartoon.

## Print answer here

# Answers

1. **Jumbles:** FRUIT LADLE FACADE JUMPER
   **Answer:** The only time some drivers obey the speed limit is when they're this—IN A TRAFFIC JAM

2. **Jumbles:** CREEL EXUDE MARKUP BURLAP
   **Answer:** A bird he should have thought of before he was knocked out—DUCK

3. **Jumbles:** AGILE GNARL MARTIN BRONCO
   **Answer:** How the so-called "coming" generation spends much of its time—"GOING"

4. **Jumbles:** DEITY ADULT FETISH BALLET
   **Answer:** What "tales" told by a long-winded bore usually have too many of—"DE-TAILS"

5. **Jumbles:** OPIUM DAUNT CLEAVE RARITY
   **Answer:** What kind of milk does an invisible baby get, naturally?—EVAPORATED

6. **Jumbles:** WAKEN OFTEN COBALT BUSILY
   **Answer:** What kind of insurance policy should a skier take out?—A "SNOW-FAULT" ONE

7. **Jumbles:** PLUME DOUGH CLOUDY BASKET
   **Answer:** When his wife lovingly gave him a shirt that was a size too small, he got this—ALL CHOKED UP

8. **Jumbles:** LUNGE RABBI GLOOMY ANYHOW
   **Answer:** He was lying in bed at night thinking of what he had been doing during the day—LYING

9. **Jumbles:** DRAMA TAKEN LAXITY CHERUB
   **Answer:** What the perfectionist had an aptitude for—EXACTITUDE

10. **Jumbles:** ALBUM SKULL KENNEL BURIAL
    **Answer:** What strange bedfellows in politics soon get used to—THE SAME "BUNK"

11. **Jumbles:** FUSSY GOURD ADJOIN DISARM
    **Answer:** What a spoiled brat does—"NO'S" HIS OWN DAD

12. **Jumbles:** WHEAT UNITY SPONGE TRUISM
    **Answer:** It's usually less than the actual cost—A "GUESS-TIMATE"

13. **Jumbles:** FELON TRYST COWARD SUBMIT
    **Answer:** At most banquets this is the main course—DISCOURSE

14. **Jumbles:** MAGIC BULLY GIBBET HOOKUP
    **Answer:** What to do if you don't like granulated sugar in your coffee—LUMP IT

15. **Jumbles:** RHYME VYING SALUTE NEWEST
    **Answer:** The constitution guarantees free speech, but it doesn't guarantee this—LISTENERS

16. **Jumbles:** OCTET VIRUS MUSEUM BALLET
    **Answer:** She married a banker because his virtues exceeded this—HIS "VAULTS" (faults)

17. **Jumbles:** CLUCK ADAPT EYELID DAMPEN
    **Answer:** Some compliments are not so much candid as this—"CANDIED"

18. **Jumbles:** BERYL KEYED ANKLET CUDGEL
    **Answer:** The first thing a man often runs into with a new car—DEBT

19. **Jumbles:** COUPE GRIPE THROAT POLICE
    **Answer:** What a successful pickpocket always tries to get next to—THE "RIGHT" PEOPLE

20. **Jumbles:** BELLE TROTH LUNACY OUTWIT
    **Answer:** All-night conversations tend to be dullest just before this—THE "YAWN" (the dawn)

21. **Jumbles:** SOOTY GULCH ASSURE JOVIAL
    **Answer:** What a Boy Scout becomes at a certain age—A GIRL "SCOUT"

22. **Jumbles:** GAILY IDIOM JUNGLE VIRILE
    **Answer:** He wouldn't be in such a hurry if he knew he was this—DRIVING TO JAIL

23. **Jumbles:** CHANT LANKY POLICY BUCKLE
    **Answer:** What the chiropractor's fees amounted to—"BACK" PAY

24. **Jumbles:** INLET MOSSY GOVERN FACING
    **Answer:** What goes on and on and has "oneself" in the middle?—AN "ON-I-ON"

25. **Jumbles:** POACH FINNY HAGGLE WEASEL
    **Answer:** What the ballplayer turned farmer found himself doing—CHASING A "FOWL" (foul)

26. **Jumbles:** ROACH STOIC LETHAL WEAKEN
    **Answer:** What the man in charge of the doughnut factory said he was—THE "HOLE" WORKS

27. **Jumbles:** BOUND DUCAT CYMBAL PREFER
    **Answer:** Another thing you can't take with you—YOUR LAP

28. **Jumbles:** PARCH EXTOL AWHILE MINGLE
    **Answer:** What tune did the teakettle whistle?—"HOME ON THE RANGE"

29. **Jumbles:** DRONE CREEK KERNEL ADRIFT
    **Answer:** The fear that relatives are coming to stay—"KIN DREAD" (kindred)

30. **Jumbles:** PRIOR GLOAT PURVEY TURBAN
    **Answer:** He was so lazy he didn't give a rap, even when this did—OPPORTUNITY

31. **Jumbles:** CYCLE GAUDY FAMILY DELUXE
    **Answer:** What that marriage counselor was always in the middle of—A MUDDLE

32. **Jumbles:** SOUSE GASSY POLISH DETAIN
    **Answer:** For that fanatic collector, this was an obsession—POSSESSION

33. **Jumbles:** KNEEL AXIOM HERALD SATIRE
    **Answer:** His footPrints on the sands of time left only this—THE MARKS OF A HEEL

34. **Jumbles:** BATCH PILOT STYLUS HEIFER
    **Answer:** Some people don't trust the ocean, because they're convinced there's something—"FISHY" ABOUT IT

35. **Jumbles:** RAVEN PIECE REVERE SIMILE
    **Answer:** Some members of the rising generation could rise even higher if they would do this—RISE EARLIER

36. **Jumbles:** FAIRY LOVER PARADE TIDBIT
    **Answer:** A deadbeat sticks to his friends until this—"DEBT" DO THEM PART

37. **Jumbles:** EXULT MUSTY SLEEPY BEHAVE
    **Answer:** What a car brings out in some men—THE BEAST

38. **Jumbles:** NAIVE KNIFE LOCALE SQUIRM
    **Answer:** He believed in marrying a woman for her figure, especially when it did this—RAN INTO MILLIONS

39. **Jumbles:** LINEN BUXOM FRACAS MALICE
    **Answer:** What they experienced when the life of the party finally went home—"COMIC RELIEF"

40. **Jumbles:** FETCH QUEUE AMAZON CANNED
    **Answer:** Fit to be eaten except in this—EDEN

41. **Jumbles:** FAVOR CLOVE NOTIFY MOTION
    **Answer:** What the bigamist took—ONE TOO MANY

42. **Jumbles:** FLUID HEDGE TURKEY POLITE
    **Answer:** What position does a monster play on the hockey team?—"GHOUL-IE"

43. **Jumbles:** LATHE CHALK HAZARD WALNUT
    **Answer:** Needs to know your zodiacal sign before she tells you this—WHAT YOU WANT TO HEAR

44. **Jumbles:** ACUTE MAIZE ZINNIA STURDY
    **Answer:** The favorite fish at that old Russian court—"CZAR-DINES"

45. **Jumbles:** MINCE ALTAR DEPUTY MAROON
    **Answer:** When the new favorite arrived at the zoo, there was this among the kids—"PANDA-MONIUM"

46. **Jumbles:** LOWLY SWISH GAIETY CAUGHT
**Answer:** "A piece of beef, and make it lean"—"WHICH WAY?"

47. **Jumbles:** SLANT HUMAN EQUITY PLAGUE
**Answer:** Another name for sarcasm—"QUIP LASH"

48. **Jumbles:** NOOSE PIPER KIMONO HERMIT
**Answer:** What she thought she'd do when her boyfriend's car needed a new muffler—KNIT HIM ONE

49. **Jumbles:** SUEDE HANDY PALACE BEFORE
**Answer:** What the intelligence agent had when he stayed home from work—A "CODE" IN THE HEAD

50. **Jumbles:** BLOAT EMPTY PARISH IMPOSE
**Answer:** What the tree that everyone gathered under was called—"POP-LAR" (popular)

51. **Jumbles:** HEAVY YOUTH TUSSLE DISOWN
**Answer:** His aptitude for platitude creates this in his audience—LASSITUDE

52. **Jumbles:** ARMOR NOTCH TALLOW MEDLEY
**Answer:** Women detest flattery, especially when it's directed towards this—OTHER WOMEN

53. **Jumbles:** HAZEL LIMBO ACTUAL RENDER
**Answer:** A fire sale is a place where bargain hunters might get this—"BURNED"

54. **Jumbles:** JUMBO TOXIC SCORCH PIRACY
**Answer:** Something often found in newspapers and on beaches—A COMIC "STRIP"

55. **Jumbles:** FATAL DIZZY INFORM PITIED
**Answer:** A surgeon might have to cut out something because the patient this—DID NOT

56. **Jumbles:** MANLY BILGE FLAXEN CASKET
**Answer:** Most people are put out when they're this—"TAKEN IN"

57. **Jumbles:** VENOM MESSY SHREWD OUTLET
**Answer:** What do you get when a monster steps on a house?—"MUSHED ROOMS"

58. **Jumbles:** JEWEL BLIMP DARING POUNCE
**Answer:** What a marriage certificate should be written on—"BOND" PAPER

59. **Jumbles:** LEAKY BURLY EYEFUL VISION
**Answer:** What were the shoemaker's two favorite kinds of fish?—SOLE & 'EEL (heel)

60. **Jumbles:** CRAZY MAKER LATEST SOOTHE
**Answer:** What loafers lack—SHOELACES

61. **Jumbles:** CREEK FUNNY VERIFY BETTER
**Answer:** They were in the process of turning on the home's power, which made it a—CURRENT EVENT

62. **Jumbles:** MUSIC SLANT QUENCH WOODEN
**Answer:** The store's window featured all-female life-size figures. One could call them—"WOMANNEQUINS"

63. **Jumbles:** JOKER CRIMP POETRY TATTLE
**Answer:** Th dogs learned to use tools so they could work on their—PET PROJECT

64. **Jumbles:** DUNCE KNACK PODIUM FACTOR
**Answer:** The circle had been sick for a while but was happy to be—UP AND AROUND

65. **Jumbles:** MOTTO SIXTH FIBULA CAMERA
**Answer:** When he said his favorite old t-shirt still fit him, it was a—BIT OF A STRETCH

66. **Jumbles:** ELUDE KNOCK SCULPT PUPPET
**Answer:** To build a submarine to reach the ocean's lowest point, it took—DEEP POCKETS

67. **Jumbles:** STYLE PROWL SUMMER FONDLY
**Answer:** The horse didn't love the idea of being urged to speed up at the—SPUR OF THE MOMENT

68. **Jumbles:** HUTCH HOIST GLADLY FIBBER
**Answer:** She opened the book about trees so she could—LEAF THROUGH IT

69. **Jumbles:** DEPTH CLOUT HUNGRY FIGURE
**Answer:** The company's new facility for producing granite and marble countertops was—CUTTING EDGE

70. **Jumbles:** BURRO NUDGE WILLOW JINGLE
**Answer:** His steak had been cooked thoroughly, which he considered a—JOB WELL DONE

71. **Jumbles:** EXUDE HIKER JOGGER BURLAP
**Answer:** When Jeanne Calment turned 122 in 1997, 121 was—HER OLD AGE

72. **Jumbles:** REUSE PANDA THWART SOOTHE
**Answer:** The house was available to lease, but the highway next to it was a—"DETER-RENT"

73. **Jumbles:** MIGHT IRONY SPLASH MADDER
**Answer:** When Richard Gere starred in the movie "Pretty Woman," he was—PAID HANDSOMELY

74. **Jumbles:** PAUSE GIVEN BATTEN PROVEN
**Answer:** The mountaintop basketball court featured—VANTAGE POINTS

75. **Jumbles:** VENUE ROUGH SMUGLY PAPAYA
**Answer:** Mount Everest tops out at 29,029 feet, making it hard for other mountains to—MEASURE UP

76. **Jumbles:** WAVER WALTZ HOBNOB NATIVE
**Answer:** The starting pitcher argued against being replaced and didn't want to—THROW IN THE TOWEL

77. **Jumbles:** METAL TITLE ODDITY GLOSSY
**Answer:** Rolex debuted in 1908 and would become known for its high-quality watches—ALL IN GOOD TIME

78. **Jumbles:** BLEND SHOVE INVENT LUXURY
**Answer:** When boxer George Foreman started promoting his grill, he became a—"SELL-EBRITY"

79. **Jumbles:** CLING KNELT HIATUS SCENIC
**Answer:** Campers at the remote campground were able to build a campfire—IN THE STICKS

80. **Jumbles:** GRIPE SHIRT APPEAR HYBRID
**Answer:** When the church at the summit was voted "Fourth Best Monument" in France, it was—HIGH PRAISE

81. **Jumbles:** OCCUR MACAW UNLOCK RUFFLE
**Answer:** After the teenager's party, his parents wanted him to clean up the—"WRECK" ROOM

82. **Jumbles:** LINER ODDLY DREAMY EXPOSE
**Answer:** The antique store was located in the basement through the—"SELLER" DOOR

83. **Jumbles:** EXPEL DITTO SKINNY VIOLET
**Answer:** The family reunion of first positive numbers featured—LOVED ONES

84. **Jumbles:** HIPPO APPLY NIBBLE SPOTTY
**Answer:** She was able to quickly reach the summit because she was—IN TIP-TOP SHAPE

85. **Jumbles:** TEPID LANKY ISLAND TIRADE
**Answer:** When they settled west of the Mississippi, their new homestead was—IN PLAIN "SITE"

86. **Jumbles:** MUNCH FABLE OUTLAW ARCADE
**Answer:** Using technology, details about the depth of the Mariana Trench have become—FATHOMABLE

87. **Jumbles:** FUDGE SALSA NEGATE SNITCH
**Answer:** When Bigfoot was spotted near the village, it—CAUSED A "SEEN"

88. **Jumbles:** FLUNG DRIFT ONWARD NOODLE
**Answer:** The initial investors in the new skyscraper were able to get in on the—GROUND FLOOR

89. **Jumbles:** ALIBI ENACT GOTTEN PUMMEL
**Answer:** The boxer was finally given a shot at the championship, and it was—"A-BOUT" TIME

90. **Jumbles:** FIFTH BEGAN SUNTAN DREDGE
**Answer:** The paramedic was trained to use a defibrillator and could use one—IN A HEARTBEAT

91. **Jumbles:** SORRY SNORT HELMET BIRDIE
**Answer:** The 5-foot-2-inch military leader got his troops to stand at attention—IN SHORT ORDER

92. **Jumbles:** SHAWL PROVE KNOTTY BEATEN
**Answer:** The audition was for the lead role, and there were plenty of actors there to—TAKE PART

93. **Jumbles:** SAVVY DRANK CUSTOM EMBARK
**Answer:** The automobile featured in Stephen King's "Christine" had—BAD "CARMA"

94. **Jumbles:** GROVE TREND BEHAVE FRENZY
**Answer:** Remember that Memorial Day is the last Monday in May and you should—NEVER FORGET

95. **Jumbles:** FILTH KOALA DEGREE BUZZER
**Answer:** Getting Penny Marshall to direct and Tom Hanks to star in the 1988 film was a—BIG DEAL

96. **Jumbles:** ABIDE FOCUS BEAGLE AGENDA
**Answer:** When the kids got too close to the rim of the Grand Canyon, their parents were—ON EDGE

97. **Jumbles:** CYNIC LOWLY GRAVEL BEHOLD
**Answer:** The company specialized in drilling for water, oil and natural gas and was—DOING WELL

98. **Jumbles:** ELOPE PUNCH DROOPY REMAKE
**Answer:** The smell of coffee brewing always—PERKED HER UP

99. **Jumbles:** SKULL AWAKE FILLET CURFEW
**Answer:** The dog was having a problem with small insects and wished he could—FLEE THE FLEAS

100. **Jumbles:** PIANO DRAFT OBLONG NUANCE
**Answer:** He's been able to understand the meaning of 1, 2, 3, etc., for a few months—AND COUNTING

101. **Jumbles:** BOOTH DECAY UNWISE LAGOON
**Answer:** When the vain guy lost his last tuft of hair,—HE BAWLED

102. **Jumbles:** TRACT BRAVO TENANT BOOKIE
**Answer:** Business at the casino was on the rise and getting—"BETTOR" AND "BETTOR"

103. **Jumbles:** LLAMA FRAUD GOALIE TANGLE
**Answer:** The gym installed some mediocre jogging machines that were—RUN OF THE MILL

104. **Jumbles:** ABOUT PLANK PICKET ACTUAL
**Answer:** When she didn't like the birthday present he gave her, he was—TAKEN ABACK

105. **Jumbles:** QUEST LOGIC TARGET SUBURB
**Answer:** For the coins in the pinball machine, it was—CLOSE QUARTERS

106. **Jumbles:** ERROR GOURD WINNER FLOPPY
**Answer:** The young flatfish were just learning to swim and were—FLOUNDERING

107. **Jumbles:** PRONG GRIPE GOPHER INVITE
**Answer:** The arm wrestling match held everyone's attention because it was—GRIPPING

108. **Jumbles:** SUSHI MERRY OPPOSE GATHER
**Answer:** It's one of the billions in the galaxy, but to us, the Sun is a—SUPERSTAR

109. **Jumbles:** AMAZE CROWD FLAUNT BOOGIE
**Answer:** The psychiatrist's new plush furniture helped to create a—COMFORT ZONE

110. **Jumbles:** SWIRL NINTH GOVERN WEASEL
**Answer:** The kids were goofing around by the back of the boat, which resulted in a—STERN WARNING

111. **Jumbles:** CHEEP SCARF UNTOLD PLURAL
**Answer:** When the forest's conifers had a party, they got—ALL SPRUCED UP

112. **Jumbles:** CAMEO SOUPY INJURE STANZA
**Answer:** Going for a stroll by the town's famous clock was a great way to—PASS TIME

113. **Jumbles:** SUEDE BLISS FELINE SHROUD
**Answer:** When she saw that the brand-new mirror was cracked, she was—BESIDE HERSELF

114. **Jumbles:** TIBIA WOULD UTMOST HOPPER
**Answer:** The attic was becoming cluttered, and his wife was no longer going to—PUT UP WITH IT

115. **Jumbles:** ELDER ELOPE POLICE UNSOLD
**Answer:** The android learned to fish by surrounding himself with—"REEL" PEOPLE

116. **Jumbles:** QUART STYLE CHOOSY STREWN
**Answer:** Einstein's handwritten memos sold for $1.8 million because they were—NOTEWORTHY

117. **Jumbles:** ICING SADLY VOYAGE APPEAL
**Answer:** Heading west from Iowa into Nebraska, they could see the prairie—PLAIN AS DAY

118. **Jumbles:** QUEEN SASSY MUMBLE REVOLT
**Answer:** To show his grandson where he bowled a perfect 300 game, they went to—MEMORY LANE

119. **Jumbles:** OFTEN GRIND SOCCER MUTINY
**Answer:** She bought the new wristwatch, and then it was—TIME TO GO

120. **Jumbles:** BLINK OUTDO TUNNEL ORIOLE
**Answer:** When the student couldn't get the microscope to work, the teacher said she'd—LOOK INTO IT

121. **Jumbles:** CHILD DOILY HEALTH NAUSEA
**Answer:** When they went hiking on the Alaskan glacier, they—HAD AN "ICE" DAY

122. **Jumbles:** SHEEP VISOR UNTRUE CAMERA
**Answer:** Two holes in one in a row! The golfers were stunned at the—COURSE OF EVENTS

123. **Jumbles:** WAIVE ODDLY WHINNY SMOGGY
**Answer:** The kids wanted to play baseball. Luckily, there were plenty of—GLOVES ON HAND

124. **Jumbles:** OUNCE GAVEL DONKEY PADDLE
**Answer:** When she signed her property over to become a park, they thanked her for her—GOOD DEED

125. **Jumbles:** JOINT SHAKY BITTER ABRUPT
**Answer:** To name the body of water Magellan traveled through, she needed to—THINK "STRAIT"

126. **Jumbles:** CURVE PHOTO FENNEL SECEDE
**Answer:** Pennies make up 1/100 of a dollar. That's—ONE PER-CENT

127. **Jumbles:** FRESH LEAKY HERBAL CANNON
**Answer:** They swam and built a sandcastle. It was going wonderfully. Everything was—"BEACHY" KEEN

128. **Jumbles:** BERET GLOAT PACIFY DRENCH
**Answer:** The new shoe company was off to a great start and taking orders for shoes—LEFT AND RIGHT

129. **Jumbles:** CANAL TACKY ABSORB IMPEDE
**Answer:** When the donkeys partied loudly on the 4th of July, it was a—"CELE-BRAY-TION"

130. **Jumbles:** WAGER CHESS STORMY TYCOON
**Answer:** Betsy Ross is credited with making the first American flag,—"SEW" THE STORY GOES

131. **Jumbles:** THIRD BLESS SQUAWK COLDER
**Answer:** To complete the painting of the golf course's thicket, the artist took—BRUSH STROKES

132. **Jumbles:** UPPER TANGY ZODIAC FIASCO
**Answer:** To eat the seagrass, the manatees—GRAZED IT

133. **Jumbles:** LINER WALTZ MADDER SERMON
**Answer:** The doctor had a rough, callous bedside manner, but he—DID MEAN WELL

134. **Jumbles:** ACUTE HONEY COERCE JOVIAL
**Answer:** Gutzon Borglum's ability to create unique sculptures allowed him to—CARVE A NICHE

135. **Jumbles:** COACH HOUSE STENCH FATTEN
**Answer:** When they started charging a toll to use the bridge, it was a—"FEE-ASCO"

136. **Jumbles:** LIVID FRONT IMPOSE WITHIN
**Answer:** She had everything she needed to apply a coat of lacquer to the table and would—FINISH IT

137. **Jumbles:** SUNNY IGLOO HUDDLE INJECT
**Answer:** When the student said, "Can I ask a question?" the teacher said—YOU JUST DID

138. **Jumbles:** AGAIN GROSS TRENCH ALWAYS
**Answer:** Making all their own low-pulp orange juice—WAS A STRAIN

139. **Jumbles:** ADAGE SURLY GOATEE THATCH
**Answer:** The problem with his ears was just wax buildup, which he was—GLAD TO HEAR

140. **Jumbles:** PRESS TRACK SMOOTH INVADE
**Answer:** The hikers hadn't seen each other in years until they—CROSSED PATHS

141. **Jumbles:** CHIDE CRUSH THRASH ENGAGE
**Answer:** How he ended up with poison ivy on his scalp was a—HEAD-SCRATCHER

142. **Jumbles:** ALPHA IMPLY ENROLL BATTER
**Answer:** He was able to understand the concept of zero seconds in—NO TIME AT ALL

143. **Jumbles:** FUSSY EVOKE MULLET HOTTER
**Answer:** The restaurant's all-you-can-eat buffet was being enjoyed—TO THE FULLEST

144. **Jumbles:** VENUE BEEFY ICONIC VANISH
**Answer:** She didn't plan on purchasing a lottery ticket, but did it—"BUY" CHANCE

145. **Jumbles:** MURKY GOOEY DENTAL BAKERY
**Answer:** He wanted to play chess but needed to get an opponent—ON BOARD

146. **Jumbles:** SUITE VALVE MUSCLE ABOUND
**Answer:** They went to view the empty apartment and were happy with the—"VACANT-SEE"

147. **Jumbles:** CARGO GUAVA CARAFE FUTILE
**Answer:** When asked if she knew what two plus two equaled, she said she knew—"FOUR" A FACT

148. **Jumbles:** SINGE DOUSE NIMBLE SKETCH
**Answer:** The tuxedo looked great on him and would perfectly—SUIT HIS NEEDS

149. **Jumbles:** VIDEO HIKER DUPLEX LAVISH
**Answer:** He wanted to buy the bookcase, but his wife—SHELVED THE IDEA

150. **Jumbles:** IMAGE EMPTY SONATA BAMBOO
**Answer:** If you get tagged while playing tag, just accept the fact and think—SO BE IT

151. **Jumbles:** POISE BEVEL MELODY SPIRAL
**Answer:** The politician's words couldn't be trusted, and therein—LIES THE PROBLEM

152. **Jumbles:** AGILE ORBIT EXCITE SOFTEN
**Answer:** In order to pinpoint the problem, the auto mechanic needed to—GET A FIX ON IT

153. **Jumbles:** GUMMY IMPEL SHRINK SALARY
**Answer:** The soldiers building the new army eating facility were—MAKING A MESS

154. **Jumbles:** FOYER NOVEL MELODY SPIRIT
**Answer:** The fishing rod and reel performed so well because they were—TOP OF THE LINE

155. **Jumbles:** UNWED LEGAL SIDING FUNNEL
**Answer:** The golf tournament began on time and was now—IN FULL SWING

156. **Jumbles:** TWINE SHINY CRAYON MIDDLE
**Answer:** Some of the mannequin parts had been used for years and were—HAND-ME-DOWNS

157. **Jumbles:** SIXTY SLANT POETIC GLOBAL
**Answer:** If you want to know if dogs are happy, look for—TELL-"TAIL" SIGNS

158. **Jumbles:** PLAID USHER MEDLEY AGENCY
**Answer:** The advertising executive was anxious to get out of bed so she could get—UP AND "AD" 'EM

159. **Jumbles:** FENCE LARVA ROTARY SUBMIT
**Answer:** The deacon introduced himself to the church's minister by saying—AT YOUR SERVICE

160. **Jumbles:** GRIME HUTCH WALRUS SOOTHE
**Answer:** They started work on the mountain tunnel and they would work until they—WERE THROUGH

161. **Jumbles:** BOTTLE OUTLAW DIVIDE BEADLE MISLAY FECUND
**Answer:** What a belly dancer can be expected to do—TWIDDLE HER MIDDLE

162. **Jumbles:** BOUNTY HELIUM CRABBY SLOGAN TALKER APATHY
**Answer:** "May I introduce you to my husband?"—"THAT'S A LOT OF BULL"

163. **Jumbles:** BELONG HAUNCH CANYON WOEFUL NOBODY FORAGE
**Answer:** Why you should get up before daylight when you're trying to find the answer to a tough problem—IT'LL SOON DAWN ON YOU

164. **Jumbles:** NOVICE AFLOAT TRYING PEWTER MATRON BRANCH
**Answer:** You should take a number at the popular pastry shop in order to keep this—YOUR "WAIT" UNDER CONTROL

165. **Jumbles:** NESTLE GALLEY FOURTH MYOPIC BUTLER HECTIC
**Answer:** Could this be another name for all the mail that's on its way to those congressmen?—"CAPITOL" LETTERS

166. **Jumbles:** IMPAIR AWHILE FIDDLE THROAT SPORTY ORNERY
**Answer:** The poker player had never gone "all in" before but was now ready to—TRY HIS HAND AT IT

167. **Jumbles:** FLINCH KARATE PLACID SHOULD RUDELY IMPORT
**Answer:** Three generations knew how to make sweaters by hand in this—"CLOTHES-KNIT" FAMILY

168. **Jumbles:** SEASON VERSUS HANDLE GARLIC POLLEN TICKLE
**Answer:** They just received more celery and asparagus, so the store employee—"RE-STALKED" THE SHELVES

169. **Jumbles:** BUCKLE EXCEED USEFUL STITCH KITTEN HAZARD
**Answer:** The boy and his dad both enjoyed bright, clear days. It was—LIKE FATHER, LIKE "SUN"

170. **Jumbles:** IGUANA SOFTLY LAVISH RITUAL ASTRAY FEISTY
**Answer:** She hung up her gold medals before the others because she wanted to put—FIRST THINGS FIRST

171. **Jumbles:** DIVIDE INFORM CANYON SEPTUM ATTAIN HAGGLE
**Answer:** Elizabeth II has been queen for 68 years, which makes her the—REIGNING CHAMPION

172. **Jumbles:** ASSIGN SESAME MURMUR ISLAND ODDEST EASILY
**Answer:** Using drones to deliver the magazines—RAISED SOME ISSUES

173. **Jumbles:** THORNY HEARTH SEQUEL BITTEN MAYHEM AFLOAT
**Answer:** Even without a personality, sodium chloride is—THE SALT OF THE EARTH

174. **Jumbles:** DUGOUT BESIDE DENOTE WEALTH FUSION DELUGE
**Answer:** After buying so many horses, the owner of the horse farm was—SADDLED WITH DEBT

175. **Jumbles:** DRESSY LATELY SHADOW PIRATE DRAGON WHIMSY
**Answer:** After the reigning hot dog-eating champion lost, he—SWALLOWED HIS PRIDE

176. **Jumbles:** ADVENT POWDER UNRULY GAMBLE DRESSY INLAND
**Answer:** He was very anxious for his fishing buddy to arrive. He was—READY AND "WADING"

177. **Jumbles:** ACCORD THROAT OBLIGE UTOPIA FUNGUS ASSIGN
**Answer:** The podiatrist had recently moved to the town and was—GAINING A FOOTHOLD

178. **Jumbles:** OUTFOX RATHER HYMNAL HIATUS MODEST PHOBIA
**Answer:** When they learned that Alfred Nobel invented dynamite, it was a—BLAST FROM THE PAST

179. **Jumbles:** INDIGO SLOWLY AVENUE GEYSER CASINO BLOTCH
**Answer:** Einstein's theories were presented in such detail because he wanted to—COVER ALL HIS "BASIS"

180. **Jumbles:** GERBIL DIGEST HUNGRY DRIVER AFLOAT UNLOAD
**Answer:** On September 6, 2020, she turned 18—IN THIS DAY AND AGE